30
Essential
Lessons
from
Psalms

Freeman-Smith, a division of Worthy Media, Inc.

134 Franklin Road, Suite 200, Brentwood, Tennessee 37027

The quoted ideas expressed in this book (but not Scripture verses) are not, in all cases, exact quotations, as some have been edited for clarity and brevity. In all cases, the author has attempted to maintain the speaker's original intent. In some cases, quoted material for this book was obtained from secondary sources, primarily print media. While every effort was made to ensure the accuracy of these sources, the accuracy cannot be guaranteed. For additions, deletions, corrections, or clarifications in future editions of this text, please write Freeman-Smith.

Scripture quotations are taken from:

The Holy Bible, King James Version

The Holy Bible, New International Version (NIV) Copyright © 1973, 1978, 1984, by International Bible Society. Used by permission of Zondervan Publishing House. All rights reserved.

The Holy Bible, New King James Version (NKJV) Copyright © 1982 by Thomas Nelson, Inc. Used by permission.

The New American Standard Bible®, (NASB) Copyright © 1960, 1962, 1963, 1968, 1971, 1972, 1973, 1975, 1977, 1995 by The Lockman Foundation. Used by permission.

The Message (MSG)- This edition issued by contractual arrangement with NavPress, a division of The Navigators, U.S.A. Originally published by NavPress in English as THE MESSAGE: The Bible in Contemporary Language copyright 2002-2003 by Eugene Peterson. All rights reserved.

The Holy Bible, New Living Translation, (NLT) Copyright © 1996. Used by permission of Tyndale House Publishers, Inc., Wheaton, Illinois 60189. All rights reserved.

New Century Version®. (NCV) Copyright © 1987, 1988, 1991 by Word Publishing, a division of Thomas Nelson, Inc. All rights reserved. Used by permission.

The Holman Christian Standard Bible™ (HCSB) Copyright © 1999, 2000, 2001 by Holman Bible Publishers. Used by permission.

Cover Design by Kim Russell / Wahoo Designs
Page Layout by Bart Dawson

ISBN 978-1-60587-341-1

Printed in the United States of America

30
Essential
Lessons
from
Psalms

Table of Contents

Introduction

Every day is a good day to praise God, but when it comes to the privilege (and the responsibility) of praising Him, some days are easier than others. After all, it isn't easy being a godly Christian in today's troubled world. Never have expectations been higher, never have temptations been stronger, never have distractions been so plentiful, and never have demands been greater. Thankfully, God stands ready, willing, and able to help you in every facet of your life if you ask Him. But it's important to remember that the best way to ask God for His help—and the best time to praise Him—is early and often.

The fabric of daily life is woven together with the threads of habit, and no habit is more important than that of consistent prayer and daily devotion to the Creator. And this book is intended to help. This text contains 30 essential lessons from the book of Psalms. During the next 30 days, please try this experiment: read a chapter each day. If you're already committed to a daily worship time, this book will enrich that experience. If you are not, the simple act of giving God a few minutes each morning will change the direction of your day and the quality of your life.

About the Book of Psalms and You

It has been called the most widely-used book of the Old Testament; it is, of course, the book of Psalms. In the Hebrew version of the Old Testament, the title of the book is translated "Hymns of Praise," and with good reason. Much of the book is a breathtakingly beautiful celebration of God's power, God's love, and God's creation.

The psalmist writes, "Let everything that has breath praise the Lord. Praise the Lord" (150:6). As Christians, we should continually praise God for all that He has done and all that He will do. For believers who have accepted the transforming love of Jesus Christ, there is simply no other way.

When is the best time to praise God? In church? Before dinner is served? When we tuck little children into bed? None of the above. The best time to praise God is all day, every day, to the greatest extent we can, with thanksgiving in our hearts.

Mrs. Charles E. Cowman, the author of the classic devotional text, *Streams in the Desert,* wrote, "Two wings are necessary to lift our souls toward God: prayer and praise. Prayer asks. Praise accepts the answer." That's why we should find the time to lift our concerns to God in prayer, and to praise Him for all that He has done.

Today, as you travel to work or school, as you hug your loved ones or marvel at a glorious sunset, think of what God has done for you, for yours, and for all of us. And, every time you notice a gift from the Giver of all things good, praise Him. His works are marvelous, His gifts are beyond understanding, and His love endures forever.

Lesson 1

Putting God First

It is good to give thanks to the Lord,
And to sing praises to Your name, O Most High;
To declare Your lovingkindness in the morning,
And Your faithfulness every night.

Psalm 92:1-2 NKJV

THE LESSON

You must guard your heart by putting God in His rightful place—first place.

Is God your top priority? Have you given His Son your heart, your soul, your talents, and your time? Or are you in the habit of giving God little more than a few hours on Sunday morning? The answers to these questions will determine how you prioritize your days and your life.

As you contemplate your own relationship with God, remember this: all of mankind is engaged in the practice of worship. Some people choose to worship God and, as a result, reap the joy that He intends for His children. Others distance themselves from God by worshiping such things as earthly possessions or personal gratification . . . and when they do so, they suffer.

> A life of intimacy
> with God is characterized
> by joy.
>
> —
>
> *Oswald Chambers*

When we place our desires for material possessions above our love for God—or when we yield to temptations of the flesh—we find ourselves engaged in a struggle that is similar to the one Jesus faced when He was tempted by Satan. In the wilderness, Satan offered Jesus earthly power and unimaginable riches, but Jesus turned Satan away and chose instead to worship God. We must do likewise by putting God first and worshiping only Him.

Does God rule your heart? Make certain that the honest answer to this question is a resounding yes. In the life of every righteous believer, God comes first. And that's precisely the place that He deserves in your heart, too.

SOMETHING TO THINK ABOUT

God deserves first place in your life . . . and you deserve the experience of putting Him there.

If God has the power to create and sustain the universe, He is more than able to sustain your marriage and your ministry, your faith and your finances, your hope and your health.

Anne Graham Lotz

Love has its source in God, for love is the very essence of His being.

Kay Arthur

It is when we come to the Lord in our nothingness, our powerlessness and our helplessness that He then enables us to love in a way which, without Him, would be absolutely impossible.

Elisabeth Elliot

When all else is gone, God is still left. Nothing changes Him.

Hannah Whitall Smith

You must never sacrifice your relationship with God for the sake of a relationship with another person.

Charles Stanley

Choose the opposition of the whole world rather than offend Jesus.

Thomas à Kempis

If we are ever going to be or do anything for our Lord, now is the time.

Vance Havner

If God is diligent, surely we ought to be diligent in doing our duty to Him. Think how patient and diligent God has been to us!

Oswald Chambers

Give God what's right—not what's left!

Anonymous

MORE FROM GOD'S WORD

And I pray this: that your love will keep on growing in knowledge and every kind of discernment, so that you can determine what really matters and can be pure and blameless in the day of Christ.

Philippians 1:9 HCSB

But seek first the kingdom of God and His righteousness, and all these things shall be added to you.

Matthew 6:33 NKJV

He said to them all, "If anyone desires to come after Me, let him deny himself, and take up his cross daily, and follow Me. For whoever desires to save his life will lose it, but whoever loses his life for My sake will save it."

Luke 9:23-24 NKJV

Let us lay aside every weight and the sin that so easily ensnares us, and run with endurance the race that lies before us, keeping our eyes on Jesus, the source and perfecter of our faith.

Hebrews 12:1-2 HCSB

Do not have other gods besides Me.

Exodus 20:3 HCSB

My Thoughts on This Lesson

_____

_____

_____

_____

_____

_____

_____

_____

_____

A Prayer for Today

Dear Lord, Your love is eternal and Your laws are everlasting.
When I obey Your commandments, I am blessed. Today, I invite
You to reign over every corner of my heart. I will have faith in
You, Father. I will sense Your presence; I will accept Your love;
I will trust Your will; and I will praise You for the Savior
of my life: Your Son Jesus. Amen

Lesson 2

Giving Thanks to the Creator

Enter into his gates with thanksgiving, and into his courts
with praise: be thankful unto him, and bless his name.
For the LORD is good; his mercy is everlasting;
and his truth endureth to all generations.

Psalm 100:4-5 KJV

THE LESSON

You have been richly and eternally blessed by the Creator.
Be thankful.

God has blessed us beyond measure, and we owe Him everything, including our constant praise. That's why thanksgiving should become a habit, a regular part of our daily routines. When we slow down and express our gratitude to the One who made us, we enrich our own lives and the lives of those around us.

Dietrich Bonhoeffer observed, "It is only with gratitude that life becomes rich." These words most certainly apply to you.

As a follower of Christ, you have been blessed beyond measure. God sent His only Son to die for you. And, God has given you the priceless gifts of eternal love and eternal life. You, in turn, should approach your Heavenly Father with reverence and gratitude.

Are you a thankful person? Do you appreciate the gifts that God has given you? And, do you demonstrate your gratitude by being a faithful steward of the gifts and talents that you have received from your Creator? You most certainly should be thankful. After all, when you stop to think about it, God has given you more blessings than you can count. So the question of the day is this: will you thank your Heavenly Father . . . or will you spend your time and energy doing other things?

> The ability to rejoice in any situation is a sign of spiritual maturity.
>
> —
>
> *Billy Graham*

God is always listening—are you willing to say thanks? It's up to you, and the next move is yours.

SOMETHING TO THINK ABOUT

Don't overlook God's gifts. Every sunrise represents yet another beautifully wrapped gift from God. Unwrap it; treasure it; use it; and give thanks to the Giver.

God is worthy of our praise and is pleased when we come before Him with thanksgiving.

Shirley Dobson

The act of thanksgiving is a demonstration of the fact that you are going to trust and believe God.

Kay Arthur

Thanksgiving is good but Thanksliving is better.

Jim Gallery

A child of God should be a visible beatitude for joy and a living doxology for gratitude.

C. H. Spurgeon

Thanksgiving or complaining—these words express two contrastive attitudes of the souls of God's children in regard to His dealings with them. The soul that gives thanks can find comfort in everything; the soul that complains can find comfort in nothing.

Hannah Whitall Smith

It is always possible to be thankful for what is given rather than to complain about what is not given. One or the other becomes a habit of life.

Elisabeth Elliot

Jesus intended for us to be overwhelmed by the blessings of regular days. He said it was the reason he had come: "I am come that they might have life, and that they might have it more abundantly."

Gloria Gaither

We all go through pain and sorrow, but the presence of God, like a warm, comforting blanket, can shield us and protect us, and allow the deep inner joy to surface, even in the most devastating circumstances.

Barbara Johnson

MORE FROM GOD'S WORD

Honor GOD with everything you own; give him the first and the best. Your barns will burst, your wine vats will brim over.

Proverbs 3:9-10 MSG

And whatever you do, in word or in deed, do everything in the name of the Lord Jesus, giving thanks to God the Father through Him.

Colossians 3:17 HCSB

It is good to give thanks to the Lord, and to sing praises to Your name, O Most High.

Psalm 92:1 NKJV

Thanks be to God for His indescribable gift.

2 Corinthians 9:15 HCSB

In everything give thanks; for this is the will of God in Christ Jesus for you.

1 Thessalonians 5:18 NKJV

MY THOUGHTS ON THIS LESSON

_____

_____

_____

_____

_____

_____

_____

_____

_____

A PRAYER FOR TODAY

Heavenly Father, Your gifts are greater than I can imagine.
May I live each day with thanksgiving in my heart and praise on
my lips. Thank You for the gift of Your Son and for the promise of
eternal life. Let me share the joyous news of Jesus Christ,
and let my life be a testimony to His love and His grace. Amen

Lesson 3

Today Is the Day

This is the day the LORD has made;
let us rejoice and be glad in it.

Psalm 118:24 NIV

THE LESSON

Today is a wonderful, one-of-a-kind gift from God. Treat it that way.

The familiar words of Psalm 118 remind us that today, like every day, is a priceless gift from God. What do you expect from the day ahead? Are you expecting God to do wonderful things, or are you living beneath a cloud of apprehension and doubt? Do you expect God to use you in unexpected ways, or do you expect another uneventful day to pass with little fanfare? As a thoughtful believer, the answer to these questions should be obvious.

C. H. Spurgeon, the renowned 19th-century English clergyman, advised, "Rejoicing is clearly a spiritual command. To ignore it, I need to remind you, is disobedience." As Christians, we are called by our Creator to live abundantly, prayerfully, and joyfully. To do otherwise is to squander His spiritual gifts.

Christ came to this earth to give us abundant life and eternal salvation. Our task is to accept Christ's grace with joy in our hearts and praise on our lips. When we fashion our days around Jesus, we are transformed: we see the world differently, we act differently, and we feel differently about ourselves and our neighbors.

If you're a thoughtful Christian, then you're a thankful Christian. And because of your faith, you can face the inevitable challenges and disappointments of each day armed with the joy of Christ and the promise of salvation.

So whatever this day holds for you, begin it and end it with God as your partner and Christ as your Savior. And throughout the day, give thanks to the One who created you and saved you. God's love for you is infinite—accept it joyfully and be thankful.

SOMETHING TO THINK ABOUT

Take time to celebrate another day of life. And while you're at it, encourage your family and friends to join in the celebration.

Christ is the secret, the source, the substance, the center, and the circumference of all true and lasting gladness.

Mrs. Charles E. Cowman

God gave you this glorious day. Don't disappoint Him. Use it for His glory.

Marie T. Freeman

Joy is the direct result of having God's perspective on our daily lives and the effect of loving our Lord enough to obey His commands and trust His promises.

Bill Bright

Submit each day to God, knowing that He is God over all your tomorrows.

Kay Arthur

Yesterday is the tomb of time, and tomorrow is the womb of time. Only now is yours.

R. G. Lee

Live today fully, expressing gratitude for all you have been, all you are right now, and all you are becoming.

Melodie Beattie

A child of God should be a visible beatitude for joy and a living doxology for gratitude.

C. H. Spurgeon

Keep your feet on the ground, but let your heart soar as high as it will. Refuse to be average or to surrender to the chill of your spiritual environment.

A. W. Tozer

Enthusiasm, like the flu, is contagious—we get it from one another.

Barbara Johnson

MORE FROM GOD'S WORD

Rejoice in the Lord always. I will say it again: Rejoice!

Philippians 4:4 HCSB

Give thanks to the Lord, for He is good; His faithful love endures forever.

Psalm 118:29 HCSB

But grow in the grace and knowledge of our Lord and Savior Jesus Christ. To Him be the glory both now and to the day of eternity.

2 Peter 3:18 HCSB

A joyful heart is good medicine, but a broken spirit dries up the bones.

Proverbs 17:22 NASB

We must do the works of Him who sent Me while it is day. Night is coming when no one can work.

John 9:4 HCSB

My Thoughts on This Lesson

_____

_____

_____

_____

_____

_____

_____

_____

_____

_____

A Prayer for Today

Dear Lord, You have given me another day of life,
and I will celebrate it. I will try to live each moment
to the fullest as I give thanks for Your creation, for Your love,
and for Your Son. Amen

Lesson 4

The Power of Constant Prayer

Therefore, let everyone who is godly pray to You.

Psalm 32:6 NASB

THE LESSON

Prayer changes things and it changes you. So pray.

"The power of prayer": these words are so familiar, yet sometimes we forget what they mean. Prayer is a powerful tool for communicating with our Creator; it is an opportunity to commune with the Giver of all things good. Prayer is not a thing to be taken lightly or to be used infrequently.

All too often, amid the rush of daily life, we may lose sight of God's presence in our lives. Instead of turning to Him for guidance and for comfort, we depend, instead, upon our own resources. To do so is a profound mistake. Prayer should never be reserved for mealtimes or for bedtimes; it should be an ever-present focus in our daily lives.

In his first letter to the Thessalonians, Paul wrote, "Rejoice evermore. Pray without ceasing. In every thing give thanks: for this is the will of God in Christ Jesus concerning you" (5:17-18 KJV). Paul's words apply to every Christian of every generation.

Today, instead of turning things over in our minds, let us turn them over to God in prayer. Instead of worrying about our decisions, let's trust God to help us make them. Today, let us pray constantly about things great and small. God is listening, and He wants to hear from us. Now.

SOMETHING TO THINK ABOUT

Pray early and often. The more you talk to God, the more He will talk to you.

Repentance removes old sins and wrong attitudes, and it opens the way for the Holy Spirit to restore our spiritual health.

Shirley Dobson

Learn to pray to God in such a way that you are trusting Him as your Physician to do what He knows is best. Confess to Him the disease, and let Him choose the remedy.

St. Augustine

When we reach the end of our strength, wisdom, and personal resources, we enter into the beginning of his glorious provisions.

Patsy Clairmont

In those desperate times when we feel like we don't have an ounce of strength, He will gently pick up our heads so that our eyes can behold something—something that will keep His hope alive in us.

Kathy Troccoli

God specializes in things fresh and firsthand. His plans for you this year may outshine those of the past. He's prepared to fill your days with reasons to give Him praise.

Joni Eareckson Tada

Obedience is the master key to effective prayer.

Billy Graham

Prayer may not get us what we want, but it will teach us to want what we need.

Vance Havner

God says we don't need to be anxious about anything; we just need to pray about everything.

Stormie Omartian

Each of us has something broken in our lives: a broken promise, a broken dream, a broken marriage, a broken heart...and we must decide how we're going to deal with our brokenness. We can wallow in self-pity or regret, accomplishing nothing and having no fun or joy in our circumstances; or we can determine with our will to take a few risks, get out of our comfort zone, and see what God will do to bring unexpected delight in our time of need.

Luci Swindoll

In the soul-searching of our lives, we are to stay quiet so we can hear Him say all that He wants to say to us in our hearts.

Charles Swindoll

MORE FROM GOD'S WORD

Rejoice evermore. Pray without ceasing. In every thing give thanks: for this is the will of God in Christ Jesus concerning you.

1 Thessalonians 5:16-18 KJV

The intense prayer of the righteous is very powerful.

James 5:16 HCSB

Therefore I say to you, whatever things you ask when you pray, believe that you receive them, and you will have them.

Mark 11:24 NKJV

I sought the LORD, and he heard me, and delivered me from all my fears.

Psalm 34:4 KJV

Rejoice in hope; be patient in affliction; be persistent in prayer.

Romans 12:12 HCSB

My Thoughts on This Lesson

_____

_____

_____

_____

_____

_____

_____

_____

_____

A Prayer for Today

Dear Lord, Your Holy Word commands me to pray
without ceasing. In all things great and small,
at all times, whether happy or sad, let me seek Your wisdom
and Your strength . . . in prayer. Amen

Lesson 5

Study His Word

Your word is a lamp to my feet and a light to my path.

Psalm 119:105 NKJV

THE LESSON

God's Word is a guide and a shield to those who trust it, study it, and obey it.

God's Word is unlike any other book. The words of Matthew 4:4 remind us that, "Man shall not live by bread alone but by every word that proceedeth out of the mouth of God" (KJV). As believers, we are instructed to study the Bible and meditate upon its meaning for our lives, yet far too many Bibles are laid aside by well-intentioned believers who would like to study the Bible if they could "just find the time."

As you establish priorities for life, you must decide whether God's Word will be a bright spotlight that guides your path every day or a tiny nightlight that occasionally flickers in the dark. The decision to study the Bible—or not—is yours and yours alone. But make no mistake: how you choose to use your Bible will have a profound impact on you and your loved ones.

> Reading news without reading the Bible will inevitably lead to an unbalanced life, an anxious spirit, a worried and depressed soul.
>
> —
>
> *Bill Bright*

George Mueller observed, "The vigor of our spiritual lives will be in exact proportion to the place held by the Bible in our lives and in our thoughts." Think of it like this: the more you use your Bible, the more God will use you.

Perhaps you're one of those Christians who owns a bookshelf full of unread Bibles. If so, remember the old saying, "A Bible in the hand is worth two in the bookcase." Or perhaps you're one of those folks who is simply "too busy" to find time for a daily dose of prayer and Bible study. If so, remember the old adage, "It's hard to stumble when you're on your knees."

God's Word can be a roadmap to a place of righteousness and abundance. Make it your roadmap. God's wisdom can be a light to guide your steps. Claim it as your light today, tomorrow, and every day of your life—and then walk confidently in the footsteps of God's only begotten Son.

SOMETHING TO THINK ABOUT

God intends for you to use His Word as your guidebook for life . . . your intentions should be the same.

The Bible is God's Word to man.

Kay Arthur

Weave the unveiling fabric of God's word through your heart and mind. It will hold strong, even if the rest of life unravels.

Gigi Graham Tchividjian

I need the spiritual revival that comes from spending quiet time alone with Jesus in prayer and in thoughtful meditation on His Word.

Anne Graham Lotz

God can see clearly no matter how dark or foggy the night is. Trust His Word to guide you safely home.

Lisa Whelchel

Words fail to express my love for this holy Book, my gratitude for its author, for His love and goodness. How shall I thank him for it?

Lottie Moon

The Bible became a living book and a guide for my life.

Vonette Bright

MORE FROM GOD'S WORD

All Scripture is inspired by God and is profitable for teaching, for rebuking, for correcting, for training in righteousness, so that the man of God may be complete, equipped for every good work.

2 Timothy 3:16-17 HCSB

For I am not ashamed of the gospel, because it is God's power for salvation to everyone who believes.

Romans 1:16 HCSB

Man shall not live by bread alone, but by every word that proceeds from the mouth of God.

Matthew 4:4 NKJV

Heaven and earth will pass away, but My words will never pass away.

Matthew 24:35 HCSB

You will be a good servant of Christ Jesus, nourished by the words of the faith and of the good teaching that you have followed.

1 Timothy 4:6 HCSB

MY THOUGHTS ON THIS LESSON

———————————————————————

———————————————————————

———————————————————————

———————————————————————

———————————————————————

———————————————————————

———————————————————————

———————————————————————

———————————————————————

———————————————————————

A PRAYER FOR TODAY

Dear Lord, the Bible is Your gift to me; let me use it.
When I stray from Your Holy Word, Lord, I suffer. But, when
I place Your Word at the very center of my life, I am blessed.
Make me a faithful student of Your Word so that I might be
a faithful servant in Your world, this day and every day. Amen

Lesson 6

The Power of Perseverance

Don't be impatient for the Lord to act!
Travel steadily along his path. He will honor you . . . .

Psalm 37:34 NLT

THE LESSON

During difficult times, you may be tempted to give up. But, God's Word makes it clear that perseverance pays big dividends.

As you continue to search for purpose in everyday life, you'll encounter your fair share of roadblocks and stumbling blocks; these situations require courage, patience, and above all, perseverance. As an example of perfect perseverance, we Christians need look no further than our Savior, Jesus Christ.

Jesus finished what He began. Despite the torture He endured, despite the shame of the cross, Jesus was steadfast in His faithfulness to God. We, too, must remain faithful, especially during times of hardship.

Perhaps you are in a hurry for God to reveal His plans for your life. If so, be forewarned: God operates on His own timetable, not yours. Sometimes, God may answer your prayers with silence, and when He does, you must patiently persevere. In times of trouble, you must remain steadfast and trust in the merciful goodness of your Heavenly Father. Whatever your problem, He can handle it. Your job is to keep persevering until He does.

SOMETHING TO THINK ABOUT

Life is, at times, difficult. When you are tested, call upon God. He can give you the strength to persevere, and that's exactly what you should ask Him to do.

Jesus taught that perseverance is the essential element in prayer.

E. M. Bounds

It is a remarkable thing that some of the most optimistic and enthusiastic people you will meet are those who have been through intense suffering.

Warren Wiersbe

Your life is not a boring stretch of highway. It's a straight line to heaven. And just look at the fields ripening along the way. Look at the tenacity and endurance. Look at the grains of righteousness. You'll have quite a crop at harvest…so don't give up!

Joni Eareckson Tada

Failure is one of life's most powerful teachers. How we handle our failures determines whether we're going to simply "get by" in life or "press on."

Beth Moore

If things are tough, remember that every flower that ever bloomed had to go through a whole lot of dirt to get there.

Barbara Johnson

God never gives up on you, so don't you ever give up on Him.

Marie T. Freeman

Instead of being frustrated and overwhelmed by all that is going on in our world, go to the Lord and ask Him to give you His eternal perspective.

Kay Arthur

Keep adding, keep walking, keep advancing; do not stop, do not turn back, do not turn from the straight road.

St. Augustine

Perseverance is more than endurance. It is endurance combined with absolute assurance and certainty that what we are looking for is going to happen.

Oswald Chambers

We are all on our way somewhere. We'll get there if we just keep going.

Barbara Johnson

MORE FROM GOD'S WORD

Brothers, I do not consider myself to have taken hold of it. But one thing I do: forgetting what is behind and reaching forward to what is ahead, I pursue as my goal the prize promised by God's heavenly call in Christ Jesus.

Philippians 3:13-14 HCSB

So we must not get tired of doing good, for we will reap at the proper time if we don't give up.

Galatians 6:9 HCSB

For you need endurance, so that after you have done God's will, you may receive what was promised.

Hebrews 10:36 HCSB

I have fought a good fight, I have finished my course, I have kept the faith.

2 Timothy 4:7 KJV

But thanks be to God, who gives us the victory through our Lord Jesus Christ. Therefore, my beloved brethren, be steadfast, immovable, always abounding in the work of the Lord, knowing that your labor is not in vain in the Lord.

1 Corinthians 15:57-58 NKJV

MY THOUGHTS ON THIS LESSON

_____

_____

_____

_____

_____

_____

_____

_____

_____

A PRAYER FOR TODAY

Lord, when life is difficult, I am tempted to abandon hope in the
future. But You are my God, and I can draw strength from You.
Let me trust You, Father, in good times and in bad times.
Let me persevere—even if my soul is troubled—and let me follow
Your Son, Jesus Christ, this day and forever. Amen

Lesson 7

Beyond Worry

Give your worries to the Lord, and he will take care of you. He will never let good people down.

Psalm 55:22 NCV

THE LESSON

Work hard, pray harder, and if you have any worries, take them to God—and leave them there.

Because we are imperfect human beings struggling with imperfect circumstances, we worry. Even though we, as Christians, have the assurance of salvation—even though we, as Christians, have the promise of God's love and protection—we find ourselves fretting over the inevitable frustrations of everyday life. Jesus understood our concerns when He spoke the reassuring words found in the 6th chapter of Matthew.

Where is the best place to take your worries? Take them to God. Take your troubles to Him; take your fears to Him; take your doubts to Him; take your weaknesses to Him; take your sorrows to Him . . . and leave them all there. Seek protection from the One who offers you eternal salvation; build your spiritual house upon the Rock that cannot be moved.

Perhaps you are concerned about your future, your health, or your finances. Or perhaps you are simply a "worrier" by nature. If so, make Matthew 6 a regular part of your daily Bible reading. This beautiful passage will remind you that God still sits in His heaven and you are His beloved child.

> Today is the tomorrow we worried about yesterday.
>
> —
>
> *Dennis Swanberg*

Then, perhaps, you will worry a little less and trust God a little more, and that's as it should be because God is trustworthy...and you are protected.

SOMETHING TO THINK ABOUT

An important part of becoming a more mature Christian is learning to worry less and to trust God more.

God is bigger than your problems. Whatever worries press upon you today, put them in God's hands and leave them there.

Billy Graham

Worry is the senseless process of cluttering up tomorrow's opportunities with leftover problems from today.

Barbara Johnson

We are not called to be burden-bearers, but cross-bearers and light-bearers. We must cast our burdens on the Lord.

Corrie ten Boom

The beginning of anxiety is the end of faith, and the beginning of true faith is the end of anxiety.

George Mueller

This life of faith, then, consists in just this—being a child in the Father's house. Let the ways of childish confidence and freedom from care, which so please you and win your heart when you observe your own little ones, teach you what you should be in your attitude toward God.

Hannah Whitall Smith

Today is mine. Tomorrow is none of my business. If I peer anxiously into the fog of the future, I will strain my spiritual eyes so that I will not see clearly what is required of me now.

Elisabeth Elliott

Worries carry responsibilities that belong to God, not to you. Worry does not enable us to escape evil; it makes us unfit to cope with it when it comes.

Corrie ten Boom

Are you serious about wanting God's guidance to become the person he wants you to be? The first step is to tell God that you know you can't manage your own life; that you need his help.

Catherine Marshall

God is bigger than your problems. Whatever worries press upon you today, put them in God's hands and leave them there.

Billy Graham

MORE FROM GOD'S WORD

Your heart must not be troubled. Believe in God; believe also in Me.

John 14:1 HCSB

Come to Me, all you who labor and are heavy laden, and I will give you rest. Take My yoke upon you and learn from Me, for I am gentle and lowly in heart, and you will find rest for your souls. For My yoke is easy and My burden is light.

Matthew 11:28-30 NKJV

So don't worry, saying, "What will we eat?" or "What will we drink?" or "What will we wear?" For the Gentiles eagerly seek all these things, and your heavenly Father knows that you need them. But seek first the kingdom of God and His righteousness, and all these things will be provided for you. Therefore don't worry about tomorrow, because tomorrow will worry about itself. Each day has enough trouble of its own.

Matthew 6:31-34 HCSB

Yea, though I walk through the valley of the shadow of death, I will fear no evil: for thou art with me; thy rod and thy staff they comfort me.

Psalm 23:4 KJV

MY THOUGHTS ON THIS LESSON

_____

_____

_____

_____

_____

_____

_____

_____

_____

A PRAYER FOR TODAY

Dear Lord, wherever I find myself, let me celebrate more and
worry less. When my faith begins to waver, help me to trust You
more. Then, with praise on my lips and the love of Your Son in
my heart, let me live courageously, faithfully, prayerfully,
and thankfully this day and every day. Amen

Lesson 8

Big Plans

Teach me to do Your will, for You are my God.
May Your gracious Spirit lead me on level ground.

Psalm 143:10 HCSB

THE LESSON

God has a plan for your life. Your job is to discover that plan
and follow it.

God has big plans for your life, but He won't force His plans upon you. Your Creator has given you the ability to make decisions on your own. With that freedom comes the responsibility of living with the consequences of your choices.

If you seek to live in accordance with God's plan for your life, you will study His Word, you will be attentive to His instructions, and you will be watchful for His signs. You will associate with fellow believers who, by their words and actions, will encourage your own spiritual growth. You will assiduously avoid those two terrible temptations: the temptation to sin and the temptation to squander time. And finally, you will listen carefully, even reverently, to the conscience that God has placed in your heart.

God has glorious plans for your day and your life. So as you go about your daily activities, keep your eyes and ears open . . . as well as your heart.

SOMETHING TO THINK ABOUT

God has a wonderful plan for your life. And the time to start looking for that plan—and living it—is now. Discovering God's plan begins with prayer, but it doesn't end there. You've also got to work at it.

God will not permit any troubles to come upon us unless He has a specific plan by which great blessing can come out of the difficulty.

Peter Marshall

A saint's life is in the hands of God just as a bow and arrow are in the hands of an archer. God is aiming at something the saint cannot see.

Oswald Chambers

God has plans—not problems—for our lives. Before she died in the concentration camp in Ravensbruck, my sister Betsie said to me, "Corrie, your whole life has been a training for the work you are doing here in prison—and for the work you will do afterward."

Corrie ten Boom

Let's never forget that some of God's greatest mercies are His refusals. He says no in order that He may, in some way we cannot imagine, say yes. All His ways with us are merciful. His meaning is always love.

Elisabeth Elliot

God cannot lead the individual who is not willing to give Him a blank check with his life.

Catherine Marshall

Our souls were made to live in an upper atmosphere, and we stifle and choke if we live on any lower level. Our eyes were made to look off from these heavenly heights, and our vision is distorted by any lower gazing.

Hannah Whitall Smith

God has his reasons. He has His purposes. Ours is an intentional God, brimming over with motive and mission. He never does things capriciously or decides with the flip of a coin.

Joni Eareckson Tada

Every experience God gives us, every person he brings into our lives, is the perfect preparation for the future that only he can see.

Corrie ten Boom

When the dream of our heart is one that God has planted there, a strange happiness flows into us. At that moment, all of the spiritual resources of the universe are released to help us. Our praying is then at one with the will of God and becomes a channel for the Creator's purposes for us and our world.

Catherine Marshall

All God's plans have the mark of the cross on them, and all His plans have death to self in them.

E. M. Bounds

MORE FROM GOD'S WORD

Who is the person who fears the Lord? He will show him the way he should choose. He will live a good life, and his descendants will inherit the land.

Psalm 25:12-13 HCSB

For You, O God, have tested us; You have refined us as silver is refined. You brought us into the net; You laid affliction on our backs. You have caused men to ride over our heads; we went through fire and through water; but You brought us out to rich fulfillment.

Psalm 66:10–12 NKJV

The steps of the Godly are directed by the Lord. He delights in every detail of their lives. Though they stumble, they will not fall, for the Lord holds them by the hand.

Psalm 37:23-24 NLT

For it is God who is working among you both the willing and the working for His good purpose.

Philippians 2:13 HCSB

We know that all things work together for the good of those who love God: those who are called according to His purpose.

Romans 8:28 HCSB

My Thoughts on This Lesson

_____

_____

_____

_____

_____

_____

_____

_____

_____

_____

A Prayer for Today

Dear Lord, I am Your creation, and You created me for a reason.
Give me the wisdom to follow Your direction for my life's journey.
Let me do Your work here on earth by seeking Your will and
living it, knowing that when I trust in You, Father,
I am eternally blessed. Amen

Lesson 9

Staying Involved in Your Church

Worship the Lord with gladness. Come before him,
singing with joy. Acknowledge that the Lord is God!
He made us, and we are his.
We are his people, the sheep of his pasture.

Psalm 100:2-3 NLT

THE LESSON

God commands you to worship Him. And, He intends for
you to be actively involved in His church. Your intentions
should be the same.

If you want to build a better life, the church is a wonderful place to do it. Are you an active, contributing, member of your local fellowship? The answer to this simple question will have a profound impact on the direction of your spiritual journey and the content of your character.

If you are not currently engaged in a local church, you're missing out on an array of blessings that include, but are certainly not limited to, the life-lifting relationships that you can—and should—be experiencing with fellow believers.

So do yourself a favor: Find a congregation you're comfortable with, and join it. And once you've joined, don't just attend church out of habit. Go to church out of a sincere desire to know and worship God. When you do, you'll be blessed by the men and women who attend your fellowship, and you'll be blessed by your Creator. You deserve to attend church, and God deserves for you to attend church, so don't delay.

SOMETHING TO THINK ABOUT

Make church a celebration, not an obligation: What you put into church determines what you get out of it. Your attitude towards worship is vitally important . . . so celebrate accordingly!

I am of the opinion that we should not be concerned about working for God until we have learned the meaning and delight of worshipping Him.

A. W. Tozer

When God is at the center of your life, you worship. When he's not, you worry.

Rick Warren

Our churches are meant to be havens where the caste rules of the world do not apply.

Beth Moore

Be filled with the Holy Spirit; join a church where the members believe the Bible and know the Lord; seek the fellowship of other Christians; learn and be nourished by God's Word and His many promises. Conversion is not the end of your journey—it is only the beginning.

Corrie ten Boom

Someone has said that the Church at its very worst is better than the world at its best.

Gloria Gaither

Churches do not lack great scholars and great minds. They lack men and women who can and will be channels of the power of God.

Corrie ten Boom

In God's economy you will be hard-pressed to find many examples of successful "Lone Rangers."

Luci Swindoll

And how can we improve the church? Simply and only by improving ourselves.

A. W. Tozer

Every time a new person comes to God, every time someone's gifts find expression in the fellowship of believers, every time a family in need is surrounded by the caring church, the truth is affirmed anew: the Church triumphant is alive and well!

Gloria Gaither

Only participation in the full life of a local church builds spiritual muscle.

Rick Warren

MORE FROM GOD'S WORD

Now you are the body of Christ, and individual members of it.

1 Corinthians 12:27 HCSB

Be on guard for yourselves and for all the flock, among whom the Holy Spirit has appointed you as overseers, to shepherd the church of God, which He purchased with His own blood.

Acts 20:28 HCSB

Then He began to teach them: "Is it not written, My house will be called a house of prayer for all nations? But you have made it a den of thieves!"

Mark 11:17 HCSB

For where two or three are gathered together in My name, I am there among them.

Matthew 18:20 HCSB

And I also say to you that you are Peter, and on this rock I will build My church, and the forces of Hades will not overpower it. I will give you the keys of the kingdom of heaven, and whatever you bind on earth will have been bound in heaven, and whatever you loose on earth will have been loosed in heaven.

Matthew 16:18-19 HCSB

My Thoughts on This Lesson

_____
_____
_____
_____
_____
_____
_____
_____
_____
_____

A Prayer for Today

Dear Lord, today I pray for Your church. Let me help to feed
Your flock by helping to build Your church so that others, too,
might experience Your enduring love and Your eternal grace.
Amen

Lesson 10

The Power of Integrity

The righteous thrive like a palm tree
and grow like a cedar tree in Lebanon.

Psalm 92:12 HCSB

THE LESSON

God's Word promises that honesty will be rewarded and dishonesty will be punished.

Honesty is the best policy, but it is not always the easiest policy. Sometimes, the truth hurts, and sometimes, it's tough to be a person of integrity . . . tough, but essential. Charles Swindoll correctly observed, "Nothing speaks louder or more powerfully than a life of integrity." Godly people agree.

As Christians we are called to walk with God and to obey His commandments. But, we live in a world that presents us with countless temptations to wander far from God's path. These temptations have the potential to destroy us, in part, because they cause us to be dishonest with ourselves and with others.

Dishonesty is a habit. Once we start bending the truth, we're likely to keep bending it. A far better strategy, of course, is to acquire the habit of being completely forthright with God, with other people, and with ourselves.

> Maintaining your integrity in a world of sham is no small accomplishment.
>
> —
>
> *Wayne Oates*

Honesty, like its counterpart, is also a habit, a habit that pays powerful dividends for those who place character above convenience. So, make this simple promise to yourself and keep it: when you're tempted to bend the truth, even slightly—or to break it—ask yourself this question: "What does God want me to do?"

Integrity is built slowly over a lifetime. It is the sum of every right decision and every honest word. It is forged on the anvil of honorable work and polished by the twin virtues of honesty and fairness. Integrity is a precious thing—difficult to build but easy to tear down. As believers in Christ, we must seek to live each day with discipline, honesty, and faith. When we do, integrity becomes a habit. And God smiles.

SOMETHING TO THINK ABOUT

Integrity pays big dividends. Deception creates massive headaches. Behave accordingly.

God never called us to naïveté. He called us to integrity…. The biblical concept of integrity emphasizes mature innocence not childlike ignorance.

Beth Moore

Integrity is a sign of maturity.

Charles Swindoll

The single most important element in any human relationship is honesty—with oneself, with God, and with others.

Catherine Marshall

You cannot glorify Christ and practice deception at the same time.

Warren Wiersbe

The commandment of absolute truthfulness is really only another name for the fullness of discipleship.

Dietrich Bonhoeffer

Much guilt arises in the life of the believer from practicing the chameleon life of environmental adaptation.

Beth Moore

MORE FROM GOD'S WORD

I will cling to my righteousness and never let it go. My conscience will not accuse [me] as long as I live!

Job 27:6 HCSB

The one who lives with integrity lives securely, but whoever perverts his ways will be found out.

Proverbs 10:9 HCSB

The integrity of the upright will guide them.

Proverbs 11:3 NKJV

May integrity and uprightness protect me, because my hope is in you.

Psalm 25:21 NIV

A good name is to be chosen over great wealth.

Proverbs 22:1 HCSB

My Thoughts on This Lesson

_____

_____

_____

_____

_____

_____

_____

_____

_____

_____

A Prayer for Today

Dear Lord, You search my heart and know me far better than
I know myself. May I be Your worthy servant, and may I live
according to Your commandments. Let me be a person of
integrity, Lord, and let my words and deeds be a testimony
to You, today and always. Amen

Lesson 11

God's Love

For the Lord is good, and His love is eternal;
His faithfulness endures through all generations.

Psalm 100:5 HCSB

THE LESSON

When all else fails, God's love does not. You can always depend upon God's love . . . and He is always your ultimate protection.

God's love for you is bigger and better than you can imagine. In fact, God's love is far too big to comprehend (in this lifetime). But this much we know: God loves you so much that He sent His Son Jesus to come to this earth and to die for you. And, when you accepted Jesus into your heart, God gave you a gift that is more precious than gold: the gift of eternal life. Now, precisely because you are a wondrous creation treasured by God, a question presents itself: What will you do in response to God's love? Will you ignore it or embrace it? Will you return it or neglect it? The decision, of course, is yours and yours alone.

When you embrace God's love, you are forever changed. When you embrace God's love, you feel differently about yourself, your neighbors, and your world. When you embrace God's love, you share His message and you obey His commandments.

When you accept the Father's gift of grace, you are blessed here on earth and throughout all eternity. So do yourself a favor right now: accept God's love with open arms and welcome His Son Jesus into your heart. When you do, your life will be changed today, tomorrow, and forever.

SOMETHING TO THINK ABOUT

God loves you more than you can imagine, and He's prepared a place for you in heaven. So celebrate God's love today and every day.

Though we may not act like our Father, there is no greater truth than this: We are his. Unalterably. He loves us. Undyingly. Nothing can separate us from the love of Christ.

Max Lucado

The springs of love are in God, not in us.

Oswald Chambers

God wants to reveal Himself as your heavenly Father. When you are hurting, you can run to Him and crawl up into His lap. When you wonder which way to turn, you can grasp His strong hand, and He'll guide you along life's path. When everything around you is falling apart, you'll feel your Father's arm around your shoulder to hold you together.

Lisa Whelchel

Snuggle in God's arms. When you are hurting, when you feel lonely or left out, let Him cradle you, comfort you, reassure you of His all-sufficient power and love.

Kay Arthur

There is no pit so deep that God's love is not deeper still.

Corrie ten Boom

The fact is, God no longer deals with us in judgment but in mercy. If people got what they deserved, this old planet would have ripped apart at the seams centuries ago. Praise God that because of His great love "we are not consumed, for his compassions never fail" (Lam. 3:22).

Joni Eareckson Tada

Being loved by Him whose opinion matters most gives us the security to risk loving, too—even loving ourselves.

Gloria Gaither

Love is not something God does; love is something God is.

Beth Moore

I love Him because He first loved me, and He still does love me, and He will love me forever and ever.

Bill Bright

The hope we have in Jesus is the anchor for the soul—something sure and steadfast, preventing drifting or giving way, lowered to the depth of God's love.

Franklin Graham

MORE FROM GOD'S WORD

For God so loved the world, that he gave his only begotten Son, that whosoever believeth in him should not perish, but have everlasting life.

John 3:16 KJV

But from eternity to eternity the Lord's faithful love is toward those who fear Him, and His righteousness toward the grandchildren of those who keep His covenant.

Psalm 103:17-18 HCSB

Praise the Lord, all nations! Glorify Him, all peoples! For great is His faithful love to us; the Lord's faithfulness endures forever. Hallelujah!

Psalm 117 HCSB

But God proves His own love for us in that while we were still sinners Christ died for us!

Romans 5:8 HCSB

Dear friends, if God loved us in this way, we also must love one another.

1 John 4:11 HCSB

My Thoughts on This Lesson

_____

_____

_____

_____

_____

_____

_____

_____

_____

_____

A Prayer for Today

Dear God, You are love. You love me, Father, and I love You.
As I love You more, Lord, I am also able to love my family
and friends more. I will be Your loving servant,
Heavenly Father, today and throughout eternity. Amen

Lesson 12

Serve Him

Serve the Lord with gladness.

Psalm 100:2 HCSB

THE LESSON

The direction of your steps and the quality of your life will be determined by the level of your service.

Jesus teaches that the most esteemed men and women are not the self-congratulatory leaders of society but are instead the humblest of servants. But, as weak human beings, we sometimes fall short as we seek to puff ourselves up and glorify our own accomplishments. To do so is wrong.

Today, you may feel the temptation to build yourself up in the eyes of your neighbors. Resist that temptation. Instead, serve your neighbors quietly and without fanfare. Find a need and fill it . . . humbly. Lend a helping hand and share a word of kindness . . . anonymously. This is God's way.

As a humble servant, you will glorify yourself, not before men, but before God, and that's what God intends. After all, earthly glory is fleeting: here today and all too soon gone. But, heavenly glory endures throughout eternity. So, the choice is yours: Either you can lift yourself up here on earth and be humbled in heaven, or vice versa. Choose vice versa.

SOMETHING TO THINK ABOUT

Wherever you happen to be—whatever your age, whatever your loss—you can find people to help and ways to serve. And the time to begin serving is now.

Before the judgment seat of Christ, my service will not be judged by how much I have done but by how much of me there is in it.

A. W. Tozer

When you're enjoying the fulfillment and fellowship that inevitably accompanies authentic service, ministry is a joy. Instead of exhausting you, it energizes you; instead of burnout, you experience blessing.

Bill Hybels

God wants us to serve Him with a willing spirit, one that would choose no other way.

Beth Moore

In the very place where God has put us, whatever its limitations, whatever kind of work it may be, we may indeed serve the Lord Christ.

Elisabeth Elliot

Through our service to others, God wants to influence our world for Him.

Vonette Bright

So many times we say that we can't serve God because we aren't whatever is needed. We're not talented enough or smart enough or whatever. But if you are in covenant with Jesus Christ, He is responsible for covering your weaknesses, for being your strength. He will give you His abilities for your disabilities!

Kay Arthur

If you want to discover your spiritual gifts, start obeying God. As you serve Him, you will find that He has given you the gifts that are necessary to follow through in obedience.

Anne Graham Lotz

Doing something positive toward another person is a practical approach to feeling good about yourself.

Barbara Johnson

If you love God enough to ask Him what you can do for Him, then your relationship is growing deep.

Stormie Omartian

Have thy tools ready; God will find thee work.

Charles Kingsley

MORE FROM GOD'S WORD

Worship the Lord your God and . . . serve Him only.

Matthew 4:10 HCSB

Therefore, get your minds ready for action, being self-disciplined, and set your hope completely on the grace to be brought to you at the revelation of Jesus Christ.

1 Peter 1:13 HCSB

If they serve Him obediently, they will end their days in prosperity and their years in happiness.

Job 36:11 HCSB

We must do the works of Him who sent Me while it is day. Night is coming when no one can work.

John 9:4 HCSB

Be strong and of good courage, and do it; do not fear nor be dismayed, for the Lord God—my God—will be with you. He will not leave you nor forsake you, until you have finished all the work for the service of the house of the Lord.

1 Chronicles 28:20 NKJV

MY THOUGHTS ON THIS LESSON

_____

_____

_____

_____

_____

_____

_____

_____

_____

_____

A PRAYER FOR TODAY

Dear Lord, in weak moments, we may try to build ourselves up by
placing ourselves ahead of others. But You want us to be humble
servants to those who need our encouragement, our help,
and our love. Today, we will do our best to follow in the footsteps
of Your Son Jesus by serving others humbly, faithfully,
and lovingly. Amen

Lesson 13

The Direction of Your Thoughts

May the words of my mouth and the thoughts of my heart be pleasing to you, O LORD, my rock and my redeemer.

Psalm 19:14 NLT

THE LESSON

Either you can control your thoughts, or they most certainly will control you.

Do you pay careful attention to the quality of your thoughts? And are you careful to direct those thoughts toward topics that are uplifting, enlightening, and pleasing to God? If so, congratulations. But if find that your thoughts are hijacked from time to time by the negativity that seems to have invaded our troubled world, you are not alone. Ours is a society that focuses on—and often glamorizes—the negative aspects of life, and that's unfortunate.

God intends that you experience joy and abundance. So, today and every day hereafter, celebrate the life that God has given you by focusing your thoughts upon those things that are worthy of praise (Philippians 4:8). And while you're at it, count your blessings instead of your hardships. When you do, you'll undoubtedly offer words of thanks to your Heavenly Father for gifts that are simply too numerous to count.

SOMETHING TO THINK ABOUT

Watch what you think. If your inner voice is, in reality, your inner critic, you need to tone down the criticism now. And while you're at it, train yourself to begin thinking thoughts that are more rational, more accepting, and less judgmental.

The mind is like a clock that is constantly running down. It has to be wound up daily with good thoughts.

Fulton J. Sheen

As we have by faith said no to sin, so we should by faith say yes to God and set our minds on things above, where Christ is seated in the heavenlies.

Vonette Bright

Every major spiritual battle is in the mind.

Charles Stanley

No more imperfect thoughts. No more sad memories. No more ignorance. My redeemed body will have a redeemed mind. Grant me a foretaste of that perfect mind as you mirror your thoughts in me today.

Joni Eareckson Tada

Attitude is the mind's paintbrush; it can color any situation.

Barbara Johnson

Your thoughts are the determining factor as to whose mold you are conformed to. Control your thoughts and you control the direction of your life.

Charles Stanley

Preoccupy my thoughts with your praise beginning today.

Joni Eareckson Tada

The things we think are the things that feed our souls. If we think on pure and lovely things, we shall grow pure and lovely like them; and the converse is equally true.

Hannah Whitall Smith

I became aware of one very important concept I had missed before: my attitude—not my circumstances—was what was making me unhappy.

Vonette Bright

It is the thoughts and intents of the heart that shape a person's life.

John Eldredge

MORE FROM GOD'S WORD

Therefore, get your minds ready for action, being self-disciplined, and set your hope completely on the grace to be brought to you at the revelation of Jesus Christ.

1 Peter 1:13 HCSB

Draw near to God, and He will draw near to you.

James 4:8 HCSB

Blessed are the pure in heart, because they will see God.

Matthew 5:8 HCSB

Dear friend, guard Clear Thinking and Common Sense with your life; don't for a minute lose sight of them. They'll keep your soul alive and well, they'll keep you fit and attractive.

Proverbs 3:21-22 MSG

Finally brothers, whatever is true, whatever is honorable, whatever is just, whatever is pure, whatever is lovely, whatever is commendable—if there is any moral excellence and if there is any praise—dwell on these things.

Philippians 4:8 HCSB

MY THOUGHTS ON THIS LESSON

_____

_____

_____

_____

_____

_____

_____

_____

_____

A PRAYER FOR TODAY

Dear Lord, I will focus on Your love, Your power, Your promises,
and Your Son. When I am weak, I will turn to You for strength;
when I am worried, I will turn to You for comfort; when I am
troubled, I will turn to You for patience and perspective.
Help me guard my thoughts, Lord, so that I may honor You
this day and forever. Amen

Lesson 14

The Power of Patience

Rest in the Lord, and wait patiently for Him.

Psalm 37:7 NKJV

THE LESSON

When you learn to be more patient, you'll make your world—and your heart—a better place.

We human beings are, by our very nature, impatient. We are impatient with others, impatient with ourselves, and impatient with our Creator. We want things to happen according to our own timetables, but our Heavenly Father may have other plans. That's why we must learn the art of patience.

All too often, we are unwilling to trust God's perfect timing. We allow ourselves to become apprehensive and anxious as we wait nervously for God to act. Usually, we know what we want, and we know precisely when we want it: right now, if not sooner. But, when God's plans differ from our own, we must train ourselves to trust in His infinite wisdom and in His infinite love.

> Waiting is the hardest kind of work, but God knows best, and we may joyfully leave all in His hands.
>
> —
>
> *Lottie Moon*

As busy men and women living in a fast-paced world, many of us find that waiting quietly for God is quite troubling. But in our better moments, we realize that patience is not only a virtue, but it is also a commandment from the Creator.

Psalm 37:7 makes it clear that we should be still before the Lord and wait patiently for Him. But ours is a generation that usually places little value on stillness and patience. No matter. God instructs us to be patient in all things, and we must obey Him or suffer the consequences of His displeasure.

We must be patient with our families, with our friends, with our associates, and with ourselves. We must also be patient with our Heavenly Father as He shapes our world (and our lives) in accordance with His timetable, not our own. And that's as it should be. After all, think about how patient God has been with us.

SOMETHING TO THINK ABOUT

When you learn to be more patient with others, you'll make your world—and your heart—a better place.

You can't step in front of God and not get in trouble. When He says, "Go three steps," don't go four.

Charles Stanley

God is more patient with us than we are with ourselves.

Max Lucado

Let me encourage you to continue to wait with faith. God may not perform a miracle, but He is trustworthy to touch you and make you whole where there used to be a hole.

Lisa Whelchel

Wisdom always waits for the right time to act, while emotion always pushes for action right now.

Joyce Meyer

How do you wait upon the Lord? First you must learn to sit at His feet and take time to listen to His words.

Kay Arthur

We must learn to wait. There is grace supplied to the one who waits.

Mrs. Charles E. Cowman

MORE FROM GOD'S WORD

Rejoice in hope; be patient in affliction; be persistent in prayer.

Romans 12:12 HCSB

Love is patient; love is kind.

1 Corinthians 13:4 HCSB

Patience and encouragement come from God. And I pray that God will help you all agree with each other the way Christ Jesus wants.

Romans 15:5 NCV

Therefore the Lord is waiting to show you mercy, and is rising up to show you compassion, for the Lord is a just God. Happy are all who wait patiently for Him.

Isaiah 30:18 HCSB

A patient spirit is better than a proud spirit.

Ecclesiastes 7:8 HCSB

MY THOUGHTS ON THIS LESSON

_____

_____

_____

_____

_____

_____

_____

_____

_____

_____

A PRAYER FOR TODAY

Lord, give me patience. When I am hurried, give me peace.
When I am frustrated, give me perspective. When I am angry,
let me turn my heart to You. Today, let me become
a more patient person, Dear Lord, as I trust in You
and in Your master plan for my life. Amen

Lesson 15

Doing What's Right

Blessed are they who maintain justice,
who constantly do what is right.

Psalm 106:3 NIV

THE LESSON

Righteous behavior invites God's blessings, and evil behavior doesn't. Behave accordingly.

As Christians, we must do our best to make sure that our actions are accurate reflections of our beliefs. Our theology must be demonstrated, not only by our words but, more importantly, by our actions. In short, we should be practical believers, quick to act whenever we see an opportunity to serve God.

English clergyman Thomas Fuller observed, "He does not believe who does not live according to his beliefs." These words are most certainly true. We may proclaim our beliefs to our hearts' content, but our proclamations will mean nothing—to others or to ourselves—unless we accompany our words with deeds that match. The sermons that we live are far more compelling than the ones we preach.

Like it or not, your life is an accurate reflection of your creed. If this fact gives you cause for concern, don't bother talking about the changes that you intend to make—make them. And then, when your good deeds speak for themselves—as they most certainly will—don't interrupt.

> Although God causes all things to work together for good for His children, He still holds us accountable for our behavior.
>
> —
>
> *Kay Arthur*

SOMETHING TO THINK ABOUT

How can you guard your steps? By walking with Jesus every day of your life.

Order your soul; reduce your wants; associate in Christian community; obey the laws; trust in Providence.

St. Augustine

He leads us in the paths of righteousness wherever we are placed.

Oswald Chambers

We have a decision to make—to turn away from sin or to be miserable and suffer the consequences of continual disobedience.

Vonette Bright

When your good behavior speaks for itself . . . don't interrupt.

Anonymous

There may be no trumpet sound or loud applause when we make a right decision, just a calm sense of resolution and peace.

Gloria Gaither

Study the Bible and observe how the persons behaved and how God dealt with them. There is explicit teaching on every condition of life.

Corrie ten Boom

The purity of motive determines the quality of action.

Oswald Chambers

Christians are the citizens of heaven, and while we are on earth, we ought to behave like heaven's citizens.

Warren Wiersbe

Life is a series of choices between the bad, the good, and the best. Everything depends on how we choose.

Vance Havner

MORE FROM GOD'S WORD

Don't be deceived: God is not mocked. For whatever a man sows he will also reap, because the one who sows to his flesh will reap corruption from the flesh, but the one who sows to the Spirit will reap eternal life from the Spirit.

Galatians 6:7-8 HCSB

Lead a tranquil and quiet life in all godliness and dignity.

1 Timothy 2:2 HCSB

Guard your heart above all else, for it is the source of life.

Proverbs 4:23 HCSB

Therefore as you have received Christ Jesus the Lord, walk in Him.

Colossians 2:6 HCSB

For this very reason, make every effort to supplement your faith with goodness, goodness with knowledge, knowledge with self-control, self-control with endurance, endurance with godliness.

2 Peter 1:5-6 HCSB

MY THOUGHTS ON THIS LESSON

A PRAYER FOR TODAY

Dear Lord, this world has countless temptations, distractions,
interruptions, and frustrations. When I allow my focus
to drift away from You and Your Word, I suffer. But, when I turn
my thoughts and my prayers to You, Heavenly Father, You guide
my path. Let me discover the right thing to do—and let me
do it—this day and every day that I live. Amen

Lesson 16

Beyond Fear

*Even when I go through the darkest valley,
I fear [no] danger, for You are with me.*

Psalm 23:4 HCSB

THE LESSON

When you feel fearful or anxious, trust God to solve the problems that are simply too big for you to solve.

A terrible storm rose quickly on the Sea of Galilee, and the disciples were afraid. Although they had witnessed many miracles, the disciples feared for their lives, so they turned to Jesus, and He calmed the waters and the wind.

Sometimes, we, like Jesus' disciples, feel threatened by the storms of life. When we are fearful, we, too, should turn to Him for comfort and for courage.

The next time you find yourself facing a fear-provoking situation, remember that the One who calmed the wind and the waves is also your personal Savior. Then ask yourself which is stronger: your faith or your fear. The answer should be obvious. So, when the storm clouds form overhead and you find yourself being tossed on the stormy seas of life, remember this: Wherever you are, God is there, too. And, because He cares for you, you are protected.

SOMETHING TO THINK ABOUT

Are you feeling anxious or fearful? If so, trust God to handle those problems that are simply too big for you to solve. Entrust the future—your future—to God. Then, spend a few minutes thinking about specific steps you can take to confront—and conquer—your fears.

When we meditate on God and remember the promises He has given us in His Word, our faith grows, and our fears dissolve.

Charles Stanley

The Bible is a Christian's guidebook, and I believe the knowledge it sheds on pain and suffering is the great antidote to fear for suffering people. Knowledge can dissolve fear as light destroys darkness.

Philip Yancey

If a person fears God, he or she has no reason to fear anything else. On the other hand, if a person does not fear God, then fear becomes a way of life.

Beth Moore

Worry is a cycle of inefficient thoughts whirling around a center of fear.

Corrie ten Boom

God shields us from most of the things we fear, but when He chooses not to shield us, He unfailingly allots grace in the measure needed.

Elisabeth Elliot

When once we are assured that God is good, then there can be nothing left to fear.

Hannah Whitall Smith

Fear and doubt are conquered by a faith that rejoices. And faith can rejoice because the promises of God are as certain as God Himself.

Kay Arthur

Whether our fear is absolutely realistic or out of proportion in our minds, our greatest refuge is Jesus Christ.

Luci Swindoll

Never be afraid to trust an unknown future to a known God.

Corrie ten Boom

Experience has taught me that the Shepherd is far more willing to show His sheep the path than the sheep are to follow. He is endlessly merciful, patient, tender, and loving. If we, His stupid and wayward sheep, really want to be led, we will without fail be led. Of that I am sure.

Elisabeth Elliot

MORE FROM GOD'S WORD

Be of good courage, and he shall strengthen your heart, all ye that hope in the LORD.

Psalm 31:24 KJV

Haven't I commanded you: be strong and courageous? Do not be afraid or discouraged, for the Lord your God is with you wherever you go.

Joshua 1:9 HCSB

Be strong and courageous, and do the work. Don't be afraid or discouraged, for the Lord God, my God, is with you. He won't leave you or forsake you.

1 Chronicles 28:20 HCSB

The Lord is my light and my salvation; whom shall I fear? The Lord is the strength of my life; of whom shall I be afraid?

Psalm 27:1 KJV

Do not fear, for I am with you; do not be afraid, for I am your God. I will strengthen you; I will help you; I will hold on to you with My righteous right hand.

Isaiah 41:10 HCSB

My Thoughts on This Lesson

_____

_____

_____

_____

_____

_____

_____

_____

_____

A Prayer for Today

Dear Lord, when I am fearful, keep me mindful that You are my
protector and my salvation. Thank You, Father, for a perfect love
that casts out fear. Because of You, I can live courageously
and faithfully this day and every day. Amen

Lesson 17

Beyond Pride

Though the Lord is great, he cares for the humble,
but he keeps his distance from the proud.

Psalm 138:6 NLT

THE LESSON

All of your talents and abilities come from God. Give Him
thanks and be humble.

Most of us aspire for the "good life." We dream of days filled with happiness and laughter, and days with little want and need. But there is some danger in the "good life." Sometimes our faith is tested more by prosperity than by adversity. Why? Because in times of plenty, we are tempted to stick out our chests and say, "I did that." But nothing could be further from the truth. All of our blessings start and end with God, and whatever "it" is, He did it. And He deserves the credit.

Who are the greatest among us? Are they the proud and the powerful? Hardly. The greatest among us are the humble servants who care less for their own glory and more for God's glory. If we seek greatness in God's eyes, we must forever praise God's good works, not our own.

SOMETHING TO THINK ABOUT

Remember that humility leads to happiness, and pride doesn't.

I can usually sense that a leading is from the Holy Spirit when it calls me to humble myself, to serve somebody, to encourage somebody, or to give something away. Very rarely will the evil one lead us to do those kind of things.

Bill Hybels

Because Christ Jesus came to the world clothed in humility, he will always be found among those who are clothed with humility. He will be found among the humble people.

A. W. Tozer

All kindness and good deeds, we must keep silent. The result will be an inner reservoir of personality power.

Catherine Marshall

We cannot be filled until we are empty. We have to be poor in spirit of ourselves in order to be filled with the Holy Spirit.

Corrie ten Boom

It was as important to me that my children be no more self-righteous than they were unrighteous. In His Gospels, Christ seemed far more tolerant of a repentant sinner than a self-righteous, self-proclaimed saint.

Beth Moore

That's what I love about serving God. In His eyes, there are no little people . . . because there are no big people. We are all on the same playing field. We all start at square one. No one has it better than the other, or possesses unfair advantage.

Joni Eareckson Tada

God exalts humility. When God works in our lives, helping us to become humble, he gives us a permanent joy. Humility gives us a joy that cannot be taken away.

Max Lucado

Jesus had a humble heart. If He abides in us, pride will never dominate our lives.

Billy Graham

Seeking after God is a two-pronged endeavor. It requires not only humility to say, "God, I need you," but also a heart that desires a pure life that is pleasing to the Lord.

Jim Cymbala

If you know who you are in Christ, your personal ego is not an issue.

Beth Moore

MORE FROM GOD'S WORD

So rid yourselves of all wickedness, all deceit, hypocrisy, envy, and all slander.

1 Peter 2:1 HCSB

Dear friends, do you think you'll get anywhere in this if you learn all the right words but never do anything? Does merely talking about faith indicate that a person really has it? For instance, you come upon an old friend dressed in rags and half-starved and say, "Good morning, friend! Be clothed in Christ! Be filled with the Holy Spirit!" and walk off without providing so much as a coat or a cup of soup—where does that get you? Isn't it obvious that God-talk without God-acts is outrageous nonsense?

James 2:14-17 MSG

Beware ye of the leaven of the Pharisees, which is hypocrisy. For there is nothing covered, that shall not be revealed; neither hid, that shall not be known. Therefore, whatsoever ye have spoken in darkness shall be heard in the light; and that which ye have spoken in the ear in closets shall be proclaimed upon the housetops.

Luke 12:1-3 KJV

Let love be without hypocrisy. Abhor what is evil; cling to what is good.

Romans 12:9 NASB

111

My Thoughts on This Lesson

_____

_____

_____

_____

_____

_____

_____

_____

A Prayer for Today

Heavenly Father, Jesus clothed Himself with humility
when He chose to come to this earth so that He might live
and die for all creation. Christ is my Master and my example.
Clothe me with humility, Lord, so that I might be more
like Your Son. Amen

Lesson 18

On Purpose

You will show me the path of life;
in Your presence is fullness of joy;
at Your right hand are pleasures forevermore.

Psalm 16:11 NKJV

THE LESSON

God has a plan for your life, a definite purpose that you can
fulfill . . . or not. Your challenge is to pray for God's guidance
and to follow wherever He leads.

Life is best lived on purpose. And purpose, like everything else in the universe, begins in the heart of God. Whether you realize it or not, God has a direction for your life, a divine calling, a path along which He intends to lead you. When you welcome God into your heart and establish a genuine relationship with Him, He will begin—and He will continue—to make His purposes known.

Each morning, as the sun rises in the east, you welcome a new day, one that is filled to the brim with opportunities, with possibilities, and with God. As you contemplate God's blessings in your own life, you should prayerfully seek His guidance for the day ahead.

> God is more concerned with the direction of your life than with its speed.
>
> —
>
> *Marie T. Freeman*

Discovering God's unfolding purpose for your life is a daily journey, a journey guided by the teachings of God's Holy Word. As you reflect upon God's promises and upon the meaning that those promises hold for you, ask God to lead you throughout the coming day. Let your Heavenly Father direct your steps; concentrate on what God wants you to do now, and leave the distant future in hands that are far more capable than your own: His hands.

Sometimes, God's intentions will be clear to you; other times, God's plan will seem uncertain at best. But even on those difficult days when you are unsure which way to turn, you must never lose sight of these overriding facts: God created you for a reason; He has important work for you to do; and He's waiting patiently for you to do it. So why not begin today?

SOMETHING TO THINK ABOUT

Discovering God's purpose for your life requires a willingness to be open. God's plan is unfolding day by day. If you keep your eyes and your heart open, He'll reveal His plans. God has big things in store for you, but He may have quite a few lessons to teach you before you are fully prepared to do His will and fulfill His purposes.

It's incredible to realize that what we do each day has meaning in the big picture of God's plan.

Bill Hybels

God has a plan for the life of every Christian. Every circumstance, every turn of destiny, all things work together for your good and for His glory.

Billy Graham

Yesterday is just experience but tomorrow is glistening with purpose—and today is the channel leading from one to the other.

Barbara Johnson

In the very place where God has put us, whatever its limitations, whatever kind of work it may be, we may indeed serve the Lord Christ.

Elisabeth Elliot

How much of our lives are, well, so daily. How often our hours are filled with the mundane, seemingly unimportant things that have to be done, whether at home or work. These very "daily" tasks could become a celebration of praise. "It is through consecration," someone has said, "that drudgery is made divine."

Gigi Graham Tchividjian

MORE FROM GOD'S WORD

Whatever you do, do all to the glory of God.

1 Corinthians 10:31 NKJV

You're sons of Light, daughters of Day. We live under wide open skies and know where we stand. So let's not sleepwalk through life . . .

1 Thessalonians 5:5-6 MSG

We look at this Son and see the God who cannot be seen. We look at this Son and see God's original purpose in everything created.

Colossians 1:15 MSG

To everything there is a season, a time for every purpose under heaven.

Ecclesiastes 3:1 NKJV

I, therefore, the prisoner in the Lord, urge you to walk worthy of the calling you have received.

Ephesians 4:1 HCSB

My Thoughts on This Lesson

_____

_____

_____

_____

_____

_____

_____

_____

_____

A Prayer for Today

Dear Lord, I know that You have a purpose for my life,
and I will seek that purpose today and every day that I live.
Let my actions be pleasing to You, and let me share Your Good
News with a world that so desperately needs Your healing
hand and the salvation of Your Son. Amen

Lesson 19

Beyond Envy

Stop your anger! Turn from your rage!
Do not envy others—it only leads to harm.

Psalm 37:8 NLT

In a competitive, cut-throat world, it is easy to become envious of other's success. But it's wrong.

We know intuitively that envy is wrong, but because we are frail, imperfect human beings, we may find ourselves struggling with feelings of envy or resentment, or both. These feelings may be especially forceful when we see other people experience unusually good fortune.

Have you recently felt the pangs of envy creeping into your heart? If so, it's time to focus on the marvelous things that God has done for you and your family. And just as importantly, you must refrain from preoccupying yourself with the blessings that God has chosen to give others.

So here's a surefire formula for a happier, healthier life: Count your own blessings and let your neighbors count theirs. It's the godly way to live.

SOMETHING TO THINK ABOUT

Feelings of envy rob you of happiness and peace. Why rob yourself?

We might occasionally be able
to change our circumstances,
but only God can change
our hearts.

—

Beth Moore

Discontent dries up the soul.

Elisabeth Elliot

What God asks, does, or requires of others is not my business; it is His.

Kay Arthur

How can you possess the miseries of envy when you possess in Christ the best of all portions?

C. H. Spurgeon

When you worry about what you don't have, you won't be able to enjoy what you do have.

Charles Swindoll

Contentment comes when we develop an attitude of gratitude for the important things we do have in our lives that we tend to take for granted if we have our eyes staring longingly at our neighbor's stuff.

Dave Ramsey

As a moth gnaws a garment, so does envy consume a man.

St. John Chrysostom

MORE FROM GOD'S WORD

Do not covet your neighbor's house . . . or anything that belongs to your neighbor.

Exodus 20:17 HCSB

Refrain from anger and give up [your] rage; do not be agitated—it can only bring harm.

Psalm 37:8 HCSB

We must not become conceited, provoking one another, envying one another.

Galatians 5:26 HCSB

For the mind-set of the flesh is death, but the mind-set of the Spirit is life and peace.

Romans 8:6 HCSB

Let us walk properly, as in the day, not in revelry and drunkenness, not in lewdness and lust, not in strife and envy.

Romans 13:13 NKJV

MY THOUGHTS ON THIS LESSON

_____

_____

_____

_____

_____

_____

_____

_____

_____

_____

A PRAYER FOR TODAY

Dear Lord, deliver me from the needless pain of envy.
You have given me countless blessings. Let me be thankful for
the gifts I have received, and let me never be resentful
of the gifts You have given others. Amen

Lesson 20

So Many Choices

Teach me, O Lord, the way of Your statutes,
and I shall keep it to the end. Give me understanding,
and I shall keep Your law; indeed,
I shall observe it with my whole heart.

Psalm 119:33-34 NKJV

THE LESSON

Every step of your life's journey is a choice . . . and the quality
of those choices determines the quality of the journey.

Life is a series of choices. From the instant we wake in the morning until the moment we nod off to sleep at night, we make countless decisions: decisions about the things we do, decisions about the words we speak, and decisions about the thoughts we choose to think. Simply put, the quality of those decisions determines the quality of our lives.

As believers who have been saved by a loving and merciful God, we have every reason to make wise choices. Yet sometimes, amid the inevitable hustle and bustle of life here on earth, we allow ourselves to behave in ways that we know are displeasing to God. When we do, we forfeit—albeit temporarily—the joy and the peace that we might otherwise experience through Him.

As you consider the next step in your life's journey, take time to consider how many things in this life you can control: your thoughts, your words, your priorities, and your actions, for starters. And then, if you sincerely want to discover God's purpose for your life, make choices that are pleasing to Him. He deserves no less . . . and neither do you.

SOMETHING TO THINK ABOUT

Your choices reveal the current level of your maturity and the current state of your faith. So choose wisely.

God expresses His love in giving us the freedom to choose.

Charles Stanley

Every day, I find countless opportunities to decide whether I will obey God and demonstrate my love for Him or try to please myself or the world system. God is waiting for my choices.

Bill Bright

Every time you make a choice, you are turning the central part of you, the part that chooses, into something a little different from what it was before.

C. S. Lewis

Life is pretty much like a cafeteria line—it offers us many choices, both good and bad. The Christian must have a spiritual radar that detects the difference not only between bad and good but also among good, better, and best.

Dennis Swanberg

Commitment to His lordship on Easter, at revivals, or even every Sunday is not enough. We must choose this day—and every day—whom we will serve. This deliberate act of the will is the inevitable choice between habitual fellowship and habitual failure.

Beth Moore

Every day of our lives we make choices about how we're going to live that day.

Luci Swindoll

No matter how many books you read, no matter how many schools you attend, you're never really wise until you start making wise choices.

Marie T. Freeman

Choices can change our lives profoundly. The choice to mend a broken relationship, to say "yes" to a difficult assignment, to lay aside some important work to play with a child, to visit some forgotten person—these small choices may affect many lives eternally.

Gloria Gaither

We are either the masters or the victims of our attitudes. It is a matter of personal choice. Who we are today is the result of choices we made yesterday. Tomorrow, we will become what we choose today. To change means to choose to change.

John Maxwell

MORE FROM GOD'S WORD

I am offering you life or death, blessings or curses. Now, choose life!
. . . To choose life is to love the Lord your God, obey him, and stay
close to him.

Deuteronomy 30:19-20 NCV

The thing you should want most is God's kingdom and doing what God
wants. Then all these other things you need will be given to you.

Matthew 6:33 NCV

If you don't know what you're doing, pray to the Father. He loves to
help. You'll get his help, and won't be condescended to when you ask for
it. Ask boldly, believingly, without a second thought. People who "worry
their prayers" are like wind-whipped waves. Don't think you're going to
get anything from the Master that way, adrift at sea, keeping all your
options open.

James 1:5-8 MSG

So I strive always to keep my conscience clear before God and man.

Acts 24:16 NIV

My Thoughts on This Lesson

_____

_____

_____

_____

_____

_____

_____

_____

_____

_____

A Prayer for Today

Heavenly Father, I have many choices to make.
Help me choose wisely as I follow in the footsteps of
Your only begotten Son. Amen

Lesson 21

Lasting Peace

*Those who love your law have great peace
and do not stumble.*

Psalm 119:165 NLT

THE LESSON

God offers peace that passes human understanding . . . and
He wants you to make His peace your peace.

Have you found the lasting peace that can—and should—be yours through Jesus Christ? Or are you still chasing the illusion of "peace and happiness" that the world promises but cannot deliver?

The beautiful words of John 14:27 promise that Jesus offers peace, not as the world gives, but as He alone gives: "Peace I leave with you. My peace I give to you. I do not give to you as the world gives. Your heart must not be troubled or fearful" (HCSB). Your challenge is to accept Christ's peace into your heart and then, as best you can, to share His peace with your neighbors. But sometimes, that's easier said than done.

If you are a person with lots of obligations and plenty of responsibilities, it is simply a fact of life: You worry. From time to time, you worry about finances, safety, health, home, family, or about countless other concerns, some great and some small. Where is the best place to take your worries? Take them to God . . . and leave them there.

> For Jesus peace seems to
> have meant not
> the absence of struggle
> but the presence
> of love.
>
> —
>
> *Frederick Buechner*

The Scottish preacher George McDonald observed, "It has been well said that no man ever sank under the burden of the day. It is when tomorrow's burden is added to the burden of today that the weight is more than a man can bear. Never load yourselves so, my friends. If you find yourselves so loaded, at least remember this: it is your own doing, not God's. He begs you to leave the future to Him."

Today, as a gift to yourself, to your family, and to your friends, claim the inner peace that is your spiritual birthright: the peace of Jesus Christ. Christ is standing at the door, waiting patiently for you to invite Him to reign over your heart. His eternal peace is offered freely. Claim it today.

SOMETHING TO THINK ABOUT

Genuine peace is a gift from God. Your job is to accept it.

The better acquainted you become with God, the less tensions you feel and the more peace you possess.

Charles Allen

A great many people are trying to make peace, but that has already been done. God has not left it for us to do; all we have to do is to enter into it.

D. L. Moody

In the center of a hurricane there is absolute quiet and peace. There is no safer place than in the center of the will of God.

Corrie ten Boom

The fruit of our placing all things in God's hands is the presence of His abiding peace in our hearts.

Hannah Whitall Smith

I believe that in every time and place it is within our power to acquiesce in the will of God—and what peace it brings to do so!

Elisabeth Elliot

The Christian has a deep, silent, hidden peace, which the world sees not, like some well in a retired and shady place.

John Henry Cardinal Newman

MORE FROM GOD'S WORD

The result of righteousness will be peace; the effect of righteousness will be quiet confidence forever.

Isaiah 32:17 HCSB

Peace, peace to you, and peace to him who helps you, for your God helps you.

1 Chronicles 12:18 HCSB

Grace, mercy, and peace will be with us from God the Father and from Jesus Christ, the Son of the Father, in truth and love.

2 John 1:3 HCSB

And let the peace of the Messiah, to which you were also called in one body, control your hearts. Be thankful.

Colossians 3:15 HCSB

Be of good comfort, be of one mind, live in peace; and the God of love and peace will be with you.

2 Corinthians 13:11 NKJV

My Thoughts on This Lesson

_____

_____

_____

_____

_____

_____

_____

_____

_____

A Prayer for Today

Dear Lord, the peace that the world offers is fleeting,
but You offer a peace that is perfect and eternal. Let me take
my concerns and burdens to You, Father, and let me feel
the spiritual abundance that You offer through the person of
Your Son, the Prince of Peace. Amen

Lesson 22

Trust God's Wisdom

The counsel of the LORD standeth for ever,
the thoughts of his heart to all generations.

Psalm 33:11 KJV

THE LESSON

God's wisdom is perfect, and it's available to you. So if you want to become wise, become a student of God's Word and a follower of His Son.

All of us would like to be wise, but not all of us are willing to do the work that is required to become wise. Wisdom is not like a mushroom; it does not spring up overnight. It is, instead, like an oak tree that starts as a tiny acorn, grows into a sapling, and eventually reaches up to the sky, tall and strong.

To become wise, we must seek God's wisdom and live according to His Word. To become wise, we must seek wisdom with consistency and purpose. To become wise, we must not only learn the lessons of the Christian life, we must also live by them.

Do you seek to live a life of righteousness and wisdom? If so, you must study the ultimate source of wisdom: the Word of God. You must seek out worthy mentors and listen carefully to their advice. You must associate, day in and day out, with godly men and women. Then, as you accumulate wisdom, you must not keep it for yourself; you must, instead, share it with your friends and family members.

But be forewarned: if you sincerely seek to share your hard-earned wisdom with others, your actions must give credence to your words. The best way to share one's wisdom—perhaps the only way—is not by words, but by example.

> If you lack knowledge, go to school. If you lack wisdom, get on your knees.
>
> — *Vance Havner*

SOMETHING TO THINK ABOUT

Wisdom is more than knowledge. Wisdom is the application of truth in such a way that it results in skillful living. Wisdom begins with a thorough understanding of God's moral order, the eternal truths that are found in God's Holy Word.

All the knowledge you want is comprised in one book, the Bible.

John Wesley

Wise people listen to wise instruction, especially instruction from the Word of God.

Warren Wiersbe

We get into trouble when we think we know what to do and we stop asking God if we're doing it.

Stormie Omartian

Yielding to the will of God is simply letting His Holy Spirit have His way in our lives.

Shirley Dobson

If you are struggling to make some difficult decisions right now that aren't specifically addressed in the Bible, don't make a choice based on what's right for someone else. You are the Lord's and He will make sure you do what's right.

Lisa Whelchel

Make God's will the focus of your life day by day. If you seek to please Him and Him alone, you'll find yourself satisfied with life.

Kay Arthur

The will of God is never exactly what you expect it to be. It may seem to be much worse, but in the end it's going to be a lot better and a lot bigger.

Elisabeth Elliot

The wonderful thing about God's schoolroom is that we get to grade our own papers. You see, He doesn't test us so He can learn how well we're doing. He tests us so we can discover how well we're doing.

Charles Swindoll

God's plan for our guidance is for us to grow gradually in wisdom before we get to the crossroads.

Bill Hybels

MORE FROM GOD'S WORD

Can you search out the deep things of God? Can you find out the limits of the Almighty? They are higher than heaven—what can you do? Deeper than Sheol—what can you know? Their measure is longer than the earth and broader than the sea.

Job 11:7-9 NKJV

For now we see indistinctly, as in a mirror, but then face to face. Now I know in part, but then I will know fully, as I am fully known.

1 Corinthians 13:12 HCSB

However, each one must live his life in the situation the Lord assigned when God called him.

1 Corinthians 7:17 HCSB

O Lord, you have examined my heart and know everything about me. You know when I sit down or stand up. You know my every thought when far away. You chart the path ahead of me and tell me where to stop and rest.

Psalm 139:1-3 NLT

MY THOUGHTS ON THIS LESSON

_____

_____

_____

_____

_____

_____

_____

_____

_____

_____

A PRAYER FOR TODAY

Dear Lord, You are my Teacher. Help me to learn from You.
And then, let me show others what it means to be a kind,
generous, loving Christian. Amen

Lesson 23

The Ultimate Protection

Cast your burden upon the Lord and He will sustain you:
He will never allow the righteous to be shaken.

Psalm 55:22 NASB

THE LESSON

Always trust God. Cast your burdens upon Him and He will protect you today and forever.

Because we are imperfect human beings living imperfect lives, we worry. Even though we, as Christians, have the assurance of salvation—even though we, as believers, have the promise of God's love and protection—we find ourselves fretting over the countless details of everyday life. Jesus understood our concerns, and He addressed them.

In the 6th chapter of Matthew, Jesus makes it clear that the heart of God is a protective, caring heart:

"Therefore I say to you, do not worry about your life, what you will eat or what you will drink; nor about your body, what you will put on. Is not life more than food and the body more than clothing? Look at the birds of the air, for they neither sow nor reap nor gather into barns; yet your heavenly Father feeds them. Are you not of more value than they? Which of you by worrying can add one cubit to his stature? . . . Therefore do not worry about tomorrow, for tomorrow will worry about its own things. Sufficient for the day is its own trouble" (vv. 25-27, 34).

> Faith does not concern itself with the entire journey. One step is enough.
>
> —
>
> *Mrs. Charles E. Cowman*

Perhaps you are uncertain about your future, your finances, your relationships, or your health. Or perhaps you are simply a "worrier" by nature. If so, make Matthew 6 a regular part of your daily Bible reading. This beautiful passage will remind you that God still sits in His heaven and you are His beloved child. Then, perhaps, you will worry a little less and trust God a little more, and that's as it should be because God is trustworthy . . . and you are protected.

SOMETHING TO THINK ABOUT

The quality of your faith will help determine the quality of your day and the quality of your life.

The Rock of Ages is the great sheltering encirclement.

Oswald Chambers

We are never out of reach of Satan's devices, so we must never be without the whole armor of God.

Warren Wiersbe

Prayer is our pathway not only to divine protection, but also to a personal, intimate relationship with God.

Shirley Dobson

A mighty fortress is our God, a bulwark never failing / Our helper He, amid the flood of mortal ills prevailing / For still our ancient foe doth seek to work us woe / His craft and power are great, armed with cruel hate, / Our earth is not his equal.

Martin Luther

As sure as God puts his children in the furnace, he will be in the furnace with them.

C. H. Spurgeon

Faith is seeing light with the eyes of your heart, when the eyes of your body see only darkness.

Barbara Johnson

Grace calls you to get up, throw off your blanket of helplessness, and to move on through life in faith.

Kay Arthur

Just as our faith strengthens our prayer life, so do our prayers deepen our faith. Let us pray often, starting today, for a deeper, more powerful faith.

Shirley Dobson

MORE FROM GOD'S WORD

Be alert, stand firm in the faith, be brave and strong.

1 Corinthians 16:13 HCSB

For whatever is born of God overcomes the world. And this is the victory that has overcome the world—our faith.

1 John 5:4 NKJV

Pursue righteousness, godliness, faith, love, endurance, and gentleness. Fight the good fight for the faith; take hold of eternal life, to which you were called and have made a good confession before many witnesses.

1 Timothy 6:11-12 HCSB

For we walk by faith, not by sight.

2 Corinthians 5:7 HCSB

I assure you: If anyone says to this mountain, "Be lifted up and thrown into the sea," and does not doubt in his heart, but believes that what he says will happen, it will be done for him.

Mark 11:23 HCSB

My Thoughts on This Lesson

_____

_____

_____

_____

_____

_____

_____

_____

_____

_____

A Prayer for Today

Dear Lord, help me to be a person of faith. Help me to remember
that You are always near and that You can overcome any
challenge. With Your love and Your power, Lord, I can live
courageously and faithfully today and every day. Amen

Lesson 24

Your Family Is a Gift from God

Unless the Lord builds a house, its builders labor over it in vain; unless the Lord watches over a city, the watchman stays alert in vain.

Psalm 127:1 HCSB

THE LESSON

Your family is a precious gift from above, a gift that should be treasured, nurtured, loved, and built upon the firm foundation of God's promises.

In a world filled with countless obligations and frequent frustrations, we may be tempted to take our families for granted. But God intends otherwise.

Our families are precious gifts from our Father in heaven. If we are to be the righteous men and women that God intends, we must care for our loved ones by making time for them, even when the demands of the day are great.

Undeniably, these are difficult days for Christian households: never have distractions and temptations been greater. But, thankfully, God is bigger than all our challenges.

No family is perfect, and neither is yours. But, despite the inevitable challenges, obligations, and hurt feelings of family life, your clan is God's blessing to you. That little band of men, women, kids, and babies is a priceless treasure on temporary loan from the Father above. Give thanks to the Giver for the gift of family…and act accordingly.

SOMETHING TO THINK ABOUT

If you're lucky enough to be a member of a loving, supportive family, then you owe it to yourself—and to them—to share your thoughts, your hopes, your encouragement, and your love.

A home is a place where we find direction.

Gigi Graham Tchividjian

One way or the other, God, who thought up the family in the first place, has the very best idea of how to bring sense to the chaos of broken relationships we see all around us. I really believe that if I remain still and listen a lot, He will share some solutions with me so I can share them with others.

Jill Briscoe

The only true source of meaning in life is found in love for God and his son Jesus Christ, and love for mankind, beginning with our own families.

James Dobson

There is so much compassion and understanding that is gained when we've experienced God's grace firsthand within our own families.

Lisa Whelchel

The truth of the Gospel is intended to free us to love God and others with our whole heart.

John Eldredge

Living life with a consistent spiritual walk deeply influences those we love most.

Vonette Bright

Live in the present and make the most of your opportunities to enjoy your family and friends.

Barbara Johnson

When God asks someone to do something for Him entailing sacrifice, He makes up for it in surprising ways. Though He has led Bill all over the world to preach the gospel, He has not forgotten the little family in the mountains of North Carolina.

Ruth Bell Graham

Calm and peaceful, the home should be the one place where people are certain they will be welcomed, received, protected, and loved.

Ed Young

A family is a place where principles are hammered and honed on the anvil of everyday living.

Charles Swindoll

MORE FROM GOD'S WORD

Choose for yourselves today the one you will worship . . . . As for me and my family, we will worship the Lord.

Joshua 24:15 HCSB

If a kingdom is divided against itself, that kingdom cannot stand. If a house is divided against itself, that house cannot stand.

Mark 3:24-25 HCSB

The one who brings ruin on his household will inherit the wind.

Proverbs 11:29 HCSB

Love must be without hypocrisy. Detest evil; cling to what is good. Show family affection to one another with brotherly love. Outdo one another in showing honor.

Romans 12:9-10 HCSB

Dear friends, if God loved us in this way, we also must love one another.

1 John 4:11 HCSB

My Thoughts on This Lesson

_____

_____

_____

_____

_____

_____

_____

_____

_____

A Prayer for Today

Dear Lord, I am part of Your family, and I praise You for
Your gifts and for Your love. You have also blessed me with
my earthly family, and I pray for them, that they might be
protected and blessed by You. Let me show love and acceptance
for my family, Lord, so that through me, they might come
to know and to love You. Amen

Lesson 25

Praise Him

From the rising of the sun to its going down
the Lord's name is to be praised.

Psalm 113:3 NKJV

THE LESSON

God deserves your praise . . . and you deserve the experience
of praising Him.

The words by Fanny Crosby are familiar: "This is my story, this is my song, praising my Savior, all the day long." And, as believers who have been saved by the blood of a risen Christ, we must do exactly as the song instructs: we must praise our Savior many times each day.

> Nothing we do is more powerful or more life-changing than praising God.
>
> —
>
> *Stormie Omartian*

Sometimes, in our rush "to get things done," we simply don't stop long enough to pause and thank our Creator for the countless blessings He has bestowed upon us. But when we slow down and express our gratitude to the One who made us, we enrich our own lives and the lives of those around us.

Worship and praise must be woven into the fabric of everything we do. Otherwise, we quickly lose perspective as we fall prey to the demands of everyday life.

Do you sincerely seek to be a worthy servant of the One who has given you eternal love and eternal life? Then praise Him for who He is and for what He has done for you. And don't just praise Him on Sunday morning. Praise Him all day long, every day, for as long as you live . . . and then for all eternity.

SOMETHING TO THINK ABOUT

All of your talents and opportunities come from God. Give Him thanks, and give Him the glory.

The time for universal praise is sure to come some day. Let us begin to do our part now.

Hannah Whitall Smith

A child of God should be a visible beatitude for joy and a living doxology for gratitude.

C. H. Spurgeon

Holy, holy, holy! Lord God Almighty! All Thy works shall praise Thy name in earth, and sky, and sea.

Reginald Heber

Praise reestablishes the proper chain of command; we recognize that the King is on the throne and that he has saved his people.

Max Lucado

Our God is the sovereign Creator of the universe! He loves us as His own children and has provided every good thing we have; He is worthy of our praise every moment.

Shirley Dobson

Praise Him! Praise Him! / Tell of His excellent greatness. / Praise Him! Praise Him! / Ever in joyful song!

Fanny Crosby

Two wings are necessary to lift our souls toward God: prayer and praise. Prayer asks. Praise accepts the answer.

Mrs. Charles E. Cowman

Words fail to express my love for this holy Book, my gratitude for its author, for His love and goodness. How shall I thank him for it?

Lottie Moon

You must never sacrifice your relationship with God for the sake of a relationship with another person.

Charles Stanley

MORE FROM GOD'S WORD

I will praise You with my whole heart.

Psalm 138:1 NKJV

Is anyone happy? Let him sing songs of praise.

James 5:13 NIV

It is good to give thanks to the Lord, to sing praises to the Most High. It is good to proclaim your unfailing love in the morning, your faithfulness in the evening.

Psalm 92:1-2 NLT

Seek the LORD while he may be found; call on him while he is near.

Isaiah 55:6 NIV

So through Jesus let us always offer to God our sacrifice of praise, coming from lips that speak his name.

Hebrews 13:15 NCV

MY THOUGHTS ON THIS LESSON

A PRAYER FOR TODAY

Dear Lord, today and every day I will praise You. I come to
You with hope in my heart and words of thanksgiving on my lips.
Let me follow in Christ's footsteps, and let my thoughts,
my prayers, my words, and my deeds honor You
now and forever. Amen

Lesson 26

Recharging
the Batteries

He makes me to lie down in green pastures;
He leads me beside the still waters. He restores my soul;
He leads me in the paths of righteousness
for His name's sake.

Psalm 23:2-3 NKJV

THE LESSON

God can make all things new, including you. When you are
weak or worried, God can renew your spirit. Your task is to
let Him.

Even the most inspired Christians can, from time to time, find themselves running on empty. The demands of daily life can drain us of our strength and rob us of the joy that is rightfully ours in Christ. When we find ourselves tired, discouraged, or worse, there is a source from which we can draw the power needed to recharge our spiritual batteries. That source is God.

God intends that His children lead joyous lives filled with abundance and peace. But sometimes, abundance and peace seem very far away. It is then that we must turn to God for renewal, and when we do, He will restore us.

> Our Lord never drew power from Himself, He drew it always from His Father.
>
> —
>
> *Oswald Chambers*

Are you tired or troubled? Turn your heart toward God in prayer. Are you weak or worried? Take the time—or, more accurately, make the time—to delve deeply into God's Holy Word. Are you spiritually depleted? Call upon fellow believers to support you, and call upon Christ to renew your spirit and your life. When you do, you'll discover that the Creator of the universe stands always ready and always able to create a new sense of wonderment and joy in you.

SOMETHING TO THINK ABOUT

God wants to give you peace, and He wants to renew your spirit. It's up to you to slow down and give Him a chance to do so.

He is the God of wholeness and restoration.

Stormie Omartian

Each of us has something broken in our lives: a broken promise, a broken dream, a broken marriage, a broken heart…and we must decide how we're going to deal with our brokenness. We can wallow in self-pity or regret, accomplishing nothing and having no fun or joy in our circumstances; or we can determine with our will to take a few risks, get out of our comfort zone, and see what God will do to bring unexpected delight in our time of need.

Luci Swindoll

The God we seek is a God who is intrinsically righteous and who will be so forever. With His example and His strength, we can share in that righteousness.

Bill Hybels

By ourselves we are not capable of suffering bravely, but the Lord possesses all the strength we lack and will demonstrate His power when we undergo persecution.

Corrie ten Boom

I have a great need for Christ; I have a great Christ for my need.

C. H. Spurgeon

In those desperate times when we feel like we don't have an ounce of strength, He will gently pick up our heads so that our eyes can behold something—something that will keep His hope alive in us.

Kathy Troccoli

God specializes in things fresh and firsthand. His plans for you this year may outshine those of the past. He's prepared to fill your days with reasons to give Him praise.

Joni Eareckson Tada

Troubles we bear trustfully can bring us a fresh vision of God and a new outlook on life, an outlook of peace and hope.

Billy Graham

MORE FROM GOD'S WORD

The One who was sitting on the throne said, "Look! I am making everything new!" Then he said, "Write this, because these words are true and can be trusted."

Revelation 21:5 NCV

When doubts filled my mind, your comfort gave me renewed hope and cheer.

Psalm 94:19 NLT

Create in me a pure heart, O God, and renew a steadfast spirit within me. Do not cast me from your presence or take your Holy Spirit from me. Restore to me the joy of your salvation and grant me a willing spirit, to sustain me.

Psalm 51:10-12 NIV

Come to Me, all you who labor and are heavy laden, and I will give you rest. Take My yoke upon you and learn from Me, for I am gentle and lowly in heart, and you will find rest for your souls. For My yoke is easy and My burden is light.

Matthew 11:28-30 NKJV

MY THOUGHTS ON THIS LESSON

_____

_____

_____

_____

_____

_____

_____

_____

_____

A PRAYER FOR TODAY

Dear Lord, sometimes the demands of the day leave me
discouraged and frustrated. Renew my strength, Father, and give
me patience and perspective. Today and every day, let me draw
comfort and courage from Your promises, from Your love,
and from Your Son. Amen

Lesson 27

Experiencing Silence

Be still, and know that I am God.

Psalm 46:10 NKJV

THE LESSON

Spend a few moments each day in silence. You owe it to your Creator . . . and to yourself.

The world seems to grow louder day by day, and our senses seem to be invaded at every turn. If we allow the distractions of a clamorous society to separate us from God's peace, we do ourselves a profound disservice. Our task, as dutiful believers, is to carve out moments of silence in a world filled with noise.

If we are to maintain righteous minds and compassionate hearts, we must take time each day for prayer and for meditation. We must make ourselves still in the presence of our Creator. We must quiet our minds and our hearts so that we might sense God's will and His love.

Has the busy pace of life robbed you of the peace that God has promised? If so, it's time to reorder your priorities and your life. Nothing is more important than the time you spend with your Heavenly Father. So be still and claim the inner peace that is found in the silent moments you spend with God.

SOMETHING TO THINK ABOUT

You live in a noisy world filled with distractions, a world where silence is in short supply. But God wants you to carve out quiet moments with Him. Silence is, indeed, golden.

Let your loneliness be transformed into a holy aloneness. Sit still before the Lord. Remember Naomi's word to Ruth: "Sit still, my daughter, until you see how the matter will fall."

Elisabeth Elliot

In the soul-searching of our lives, we are to stay quiet so we can hear Him say all that He wants to say to us in our hearts.

Charles Swindoll

Because Jesus Christ is our Great High Priest, not only can we approach God without a human "go-between," we can also hear and learn from God in some sacred moments without one.

Beth Moore

Among the enemies to devotion, none is so harmful as distractions. Whatever excites the curiosity, scatters the thoughts, disquiets the heart, absorbs the interests, or shifts our life focus from the kingdom of God within us to the world around us—that is a distraction; and the world is full of them.

A. W. Tozer

Growth takes place in quietness, in hidden ways, in silence and solitude. The process is not accessible to observation.

Eugene Peterson

Noise and words and frenzied, hectic schedules dull our senses, closing our ears to His still, small voice and making us numb to His touch.

Charles Swindoll

It is in that stillness that the Voice will be heard, the only voice in all the universe that speaks peace to the deepest part of us.

Elisabeth Elliot

Instead of waiting for the feeling, wait upon God. You can do this by growing still and quiet, then expressing in prayer what your mind knows is true about Him, even if your heart doesn't feel it at this moment.

Shirley Dobson

When we are in the presence of God, removed from distractions, we are able to hear him more clearly, and a secure environment has been established for the young and broken places in our hearts to surface.

John Eldredge

The remedy for distractions is the same now as it was in earlier and simpler times: prayer, meditation, and the cultivation of the inner life.

A. W. Tozer

MORE FROM GOD'S WORD

Be silent before the Lord and wait expectantly for Him.

Psalm 37:7 HCSB

Truly my soul silently waits for God; from Him comes my salvation.

Psalm 62:1 NKJV

My soul, wait silently for God alone, for my expectation is from Him.

Psalm 62:5 NKJV

Be silent before Me.

Isaiah 41:1 HCSB

A simple life in the Fear-of-God is better than a rich life with a ton of headaches.

Proverbs 15:16 MSG

My Thoughts on This Lesson

_____

_____

_____

_____

_____

_____

_____

_____

_____

_____

A Prayer for Today

Dear Lord, help me remember the importance of silence.
Help me discover quiet moments throughout the day so that
I can sense Your presence and Your love. Amen

Lesson 28

Finding Strength

Be of good courage,
And He shall strengthen your heart,
All you who hope in the Lord.

Psalm 31:24 NKJV

THE LESSON

When you are tired, fearful, or discouraged, God can restore your strength.

Where do you go to find strength? The gym? The health food store? The espresso bar? There's a better source of strength, of course, and that source is God. He is a never-ending source of strength and courage if you call upon Him.

Are you an energized Christian? You should be. But if you're not, you must seek strength and renewal from the source that will never fail: that source, of course, is your Heavenly Father. And rest assured—when you sincerely petition Him, He will give you all the strength you need to live victoriously for Him.

Have you "tapped in" to the power of God? Have you turned your life and your heart over to Him, or are you muddling along under your own power? The answer to this question will determine the quality of your life here on earth and the destiny of your life throughout all eternity. So start tapping in—and remember that when it comes to strength, God is the Ultimate Source.

SOMETHING TO THINK ABOUT

Need strength? Slow down, get more rest, engage in sensible exercise, and turn your troubles over to God . . . . but not necessarily in that order.

When the dream of our heart is one that God has planted there, a strange happiness flows into us. At that moment, all of the spiritual resources of the universe are released to help us. Our praying is then at one with the will of God and becomes a channel for the Creator's purposes for us and our world.

Catherine Marshall

Worry does not empty tomorrow of its sorrow; it empties today of its strength.

Corrie ten Boom

God is great and God is powerful, but we must invite him to be powerful in our lives. His strength is always there, but it's up to us to provide a channel through which that power can flow.

Bill Hybels

If we take God's program, we can have God's power—not otherwise.

E. Stanley Jones

If you are weak, limited, ordinary, you are the best material through which God can work!

Henry Blackaby and Claude King

Sometimes I think spiritual and physical strength is like manna: you get just what you need for the day, no more.

Suzanne Dale Ezell

When you and I are related to Jesus Christ, our strength and wisdom and peace and joy and love and hope may run out, but His life rushes in to keep us filled to the brim. We are showered with blessings, not because of anything we have or have not done, but simply because of Him.

Anne Graham Lotz

We are never stronger than the moment we admit we are weak.

Beth Moore

God gives us always strength enough, and sense enough, for everything he wants us to do.

John Ruskin

The same God who empowered Samson, Gideon, and Paul seeks to empower my life and your life, because God hasn't changed.

Bill Hybels

MORE FROM GOD'S WORD

Be of good courage, and let us be strong for our people and for the cities of our God. And may the Lord do what is good in His sight.

1 Chronicles 19:13 NKJV

Do you not know? Have you not heard? The Everlasting God, the LORD, the Creator of the ends of the earth does not become weary or tired. His understanding is inscrutable. He gives strength to the weary, and to him who lacks might He increases power. Though youths grow weary and tired, and vigorous young men stumble badly, yet those who wait for the LORD will gain new strength; they will mount up with wings like eagles, they will run and not get tired, they will walk and not become weary.

Isaiah 40:28–31 NASB

He said unto me, My grace is sufficient for thee: for my strength is made perfect in weakness.

2 Corinthians 12:9 KJV

The LORD is my strength and my song . . . .

Exodus 15:2 NIV

I am able to do all things through Him who strengthens me.

Philippians 4:13 HCSB

My Thoughts on This Lesson

_____

_____

_____

_____

_____

_____

_____

_____

A Prayer for Today

Dear Lord, whenever I feel discouraged or tired, I will turn
to You for strength. I know that when I open my heart to You,
Father, You will renew my strength and my enthusiasm.
Let Your will be my will, Lord, and let me find
my strength in You. Amen

Lesson 29

Do You Believe in Miracles?

You are the God who works wonders;
You revealed Your strength among the peoples.
Psalm 77:14 HCSB

THE LESSON

God does miraculous things. So, never be afraid to ask for a miracle.

If you haven't seen any of God's miracles lately, you haven't been looking. Throughout history, the Creator has intervened in the course of human events in ways that cannot be explained by science or human rationale. And He's still doing so today.

God's miracles are not limited to special occasions, nor are they witnessed by a select few. God is crafting His wonders all around us: the miracle of the birth of a new baby; the miracle of a world renewing itself with every sunrise; the miracle of lives transformed by God's love and grace. Each day, God's handiwork is evident for all to see and experience.

Today, seize the opportunity to inspect God's hand at work. His miracles come in a variety of shapes and sizes, so keep your eyes and your heart open. Be watchful, and you'll soon be amazed.

SOMETHING TO THINK ABOUT

God has infinite power. If you're watchful, you'll observe many miracles. So keep your eyes, your heart, and your mind open.

When we face an impossible situation, all self-reliance and self-confidence must melt away; we must be totally dependent on Him for the resources.

Anne Graham Lotz

There is Someone who makes possible what seems completely impossible.

Catherine Marshall

Only God can move mountains, but faith and prayer can move God.

E. M. Bounds

Miracles broke the physical laws of the universe; forgiveness broke the moral rules.

Philip Yancey

The impossible is exactly what God does.

Oswald Chambers

Are you looking for a miracle? If you keep your eyes wide open and trust in God, you won't have to look very far.

Marie T. Freeman

Prayer succeeds
when all else fails.

—

E. M. Bounds

MORE FROM GOD'S WORD

Looking at them, Jesus said, "With men it is impossible, but not with God, because all things are possible with God."

Mark 10:27 HCSB

But as it is written: "Eye has not seen, nor ear heard, nor have entered into the heart of man the things which God has prepared for those who love Him."

1 Corinthians 2:9 NKJV

I assure you: The one who believes in Me will also do the works that I do. And he will do even greater works than these, because I am going to the Father.

John 14:12 HCSB

Ah, Lord God! Behold, You have made the heavens and the earth by Your great power and outstretched arm. There is nothing too hard for You.

Jeremiah 32:17 NKJV

For nothing will be impossible with God.

Luke 1:37 HCSB

MY THOUGHTS ON THIS LESSON

_____

_____

_____

_____

_____

_____

_____

_____

_____

A PRAYER FOR TODAY

Dear God, nothing is impossible for You. Your infinite power is
beyond human understanding—keep me always mindful of Your
strength. When I lose hope, give me faith; when others lose hope,
let me tell them of Your glory and Your works. Today, Lord,
let me expect the miraculous, and let me trust in You. Amen

Lesson 30

Your Very Bright Future

Praise the Lord, all nations! Glorify Him, all peoples!
For great is His faithful love to us;
the Lord's faithfulness endures forever. Hallelujah!

Psalm 117 HCSB

THE LESSON

Even when the world seems dark, the future is bright for those who love the Lord.

Because we are saved by a risen Christ, we can have hope for the future, no matter how troublesome our present circumstances may seem. After all, God has promised that we are His throughout eternity. And, He has told us that we must place our hopes in Him.

Of course, we will face disappointments and failures while we are here on earth, but these are only temporary defeats. This world can be a place of trials and tribulations, but when we place our trust in the Giver of all things good, we are secure. God has promised us peace, joy, and eternal life. And God keeps His promises today, tomorrow, and forever.

> Take courage.
> We walk in the
> wilderness today and
> in the Promised Land
> tomorrow.
>
> —
>
> *D. L. Moody*

Are you willing to place your future in the hands of a loving and all-knowing God? Do you trust in the ultimate goodness of His plan for your life? Will you face today's challenges with optimism and hope? You should. After all, God created you for a very important purpose: His purpose. And you still have important work to do: His work.

Today, as you live in the present and look to the future, remember that God has a plan for you. Act—and believe—accordingly.

SOMETHING TO THINK ABOUT

Your future depends, to a very great extent, upon you. So keep learning and keep growing personally, intellectually, emotionally, and spiritually.

You can look forward with hope, because one day there will be no more separation, no more scars, and no more suffering in My Father's House. It's the home of your dreams!

Anne Graham Lotz

The Christian believes in a fabulous future.

Billy Graham

We spend our lives dreaming of the future, not realizing that a little of it slips away every day.

Barbara Johnson

Our future may look fearfully intimidating, yet we can look up to the Engineer of the Universe, confident that nothing escapes His attention or slips out of the control of those strong hands.

Elisabeth Elliot

The best we can hope for in this life is a knothole peek at the shining realities ahead. Yet a glimpse is enough. It's enough to convince our hearts that whatever sufferings and sorrows currently assail us aren't worthy of comparison to that which waits over the horizon.

Joni Eareckson Tada

Yesterday is just experience but tomorrow is glistening with purpose—and today is the channel leading from one to the other.

Barbara Johnson

Do not limit the limitless God! With Him, face the future unafraid because you are never alone.

Mrs. Charles E. Cowman

No matter how heavy the burden, daily strength is given, so I expect we need not give ourselves any concern as to what the outcome will be. We must simply go forward.

Annie Armstrong

MORE FROM GOD'S WORD

Blessed be the God and Father of our Lord Jesus Christ, who according to His abundant mercy has begotten us again to a living hope through the resurrection of Jesus Christ from the dead . . . .

1 Peter 1:3 NKJV

Wisdom is pleasing to you. If you find it, you have hope for the future.

Proverbs 24:14 NCV

When you are in distress and all these things have happened to you, you will return to the Lord your God in later days and obey Him. He will not leave you, destroy you, or forget the covenant with your fathers that He swore to them by oath, because the Lord your God is a compassionate God.

Deuteronomy 4:30-31 HCSB

But if we hope for what we do not see, we eagerly wait for it with patience.

Romans 8:25 HCSB

"For I know the plans I have for you"—[this is] the Lord's declaration— "plans for [your] welfare, not for disaster, to give you a future and a hope."

Jeremiah 29:11 HCSB

My Thoughts on This Lesson

_____

_____

_____

_____

_____

_____

_____

_____

_____

A Prayer for Today

Dear Lord, as I look to the future, I will place my trust in You.
If I become discouraged, I will turn to You. If I am afraid, I will
seek strength in You. You are my Father, and I will place
my hope, my trust, and my faith in You. Amen

More from God's Word

Following Christ

Then He said to them all, *"If anyone wants to come with Me, he must deny himself, take up his cross daily, and follow Me."*

Luke 9:23 HCSB

For I have given you an example that you also should do just as I have done for you.

John 13:15 HCSB

No one can be a slave of two masters, since either he will hate one and love the other, or be devoted to one and despise the other. You cannot be slaves of God and of money.

Matthew 6:24 HCSB

Anyone finding his life will lose it, and anyone losing his life because of Me will find it.

Matthew 10:39 HCSB

If anyone serves Me, let him follow Me; and where I am, there My servant will be also. If anyone serves Me, him My Father will honor.

John 12:26 NKJV

My cup runs over.
Surely goodness and mercy
shall follow me all the days of my life;
and I will dwell in the house
of the Lord forever.

—

Psalm 23:5-6 NKJV

Hope

I wait for the Lord, my soul waits, and in His word I do hope. My soul waits for the Lord more than those who watch for the morning—yes, more than those who watch for the morning.

Psalm 130:5-6 NKJV

Let us hold on to the confession of our hope without wavering, for He who promised is faithful.

Hebrews 10:23 HCSB

For in You, O Lord, I hope; You will hear, O Lord my God.

Psalm 38:15 NKJV

The Lord is good to those who wait for Him, to the soul who seeks Him. It is good that one should hope and wait quietly for the salvation of the Lord.

Lamentations 3:25-26 NKJV

Now may the God of hope fill you with all joy and peace in believing, so that you may overflow with hope by the power of the Holy Spirit.

Romans 15:13 HCSB

Blessings

You will show me the path of life; in Your presence is fullness of joy; at Your right hand are pleasures forevermore.

Psalm 16:11 NKJV

I will make them and the area around My hill a blessing: I will send down showers in their season—showers of blessing.

Ezekiel 34:26 HCSB

Obey My voice, and I will be your God, and you shall be my people. And walk in all the ways that I have commanded you, that it may be well with you.

Jeremiah 7:23 NKJV

The Lord bless you and keep you; the Lord make His face shine upon you, and be gracious to you.

Numbers 6:24-25 NKJV

Blessed is a man who endures trials, because when he passes the test he will receive the crown of life that He has promised to those who love Him.

James 1:12 HCSB

Adversity

When you are in distress and all these things have happened to you, you will return to the Lord your God in later days and obey Him. He will not leave you, destroy you, or forget the covenant with your fathers that He swore to them by oath, because the Lord your God is a compassionate God.

Deuteronomy 4:30-31 HCSB

Whatever has been born of God conquers the world. This is the victory that has conquered the world: our faith.

1 John 5:4 HCSB

Dear friends, when the fiery ordeal arises among you to test you, don't be surprised by it, as if something unusual were happening to you. Instead, as you share in the sufferings of the Messiah rejoice, so that you may also rejoice with great joy at the revelation of His glory.

1 Peter 4:12-13 HCSB

We are pressured in every way but not crushed; we are perplexed but not in despair.

2 Corinthians 4:8 HCSB

God is our refuge and strength,
a very present help in trouble.

—

Psalm 46:1 NKJV

Evil

Therefore, submit to God. But resist the Devil, and he will flee from you. Draw near to God, and He will draw near to you. Cleanse your hands, sinners, and purify your hearts, double-minded people!

James 4:7-8 HCSB

Do not be conquered by evil, but conquer evil with good.

Romans 12:21 HCSB

For everyone who practices wicked things hates the light and avoids it, so that his deeds may not be exposed. But anyone who lives by the truth comes to the light, so that his works may be shown to be accomplished by God.

John 3:20–21 HCSB

He replied, "Every plant that My heavenly Father didn't plant will be uprooted."

Matthew 15:13 HCSB

But the path of the just is like the shining sun, that shines ever brighter unto the perfect day. The way of the wicked is like darkness; they do not know what makes them stumble.

Proverbs 4:18-19 NKJV

Don't consider yourself to be wise;
fear the Lord
and turn away from evil.

—

Proverbs 3:7 HCSB

Fearing God

Don't consider yourself to be wise; fear the Lord and turn away from evil.

Proverbs 3:7 HCSB

The fear of the Lord is the beginning of knowledge, but fools despise wisdom and instruction.

Proverbs 1:7 NKJV

The fear of the Lord is the beginning of wisdom, and the knowledge of the Holy One is understanding.

Proverbs 9:10 HCSB

The fear of the Lord is the beginning of wisdom; all who follow His instructions have good insight.

Psalm 111:10 HCSB

The fear of the Lord is a fountain of life, turning people from the snares of death.

Proverbs 14:27 HCSB

To fear the Lord is to hate evil.

—

Proverbs 8:13 HCSB

God's Presence

Draw near to God, and He will draw near to you.

James 4:8 HCSB

You will seek Me and find Me when you search for Me with all your heart.

Jeremiah 29:13 HCSB

The Lord is near all who call out to Him, all who call out to Him with integrity. He fulfills the desires of those who fear Him; He hears their cry for help and saves them.

Psalm 145:18-19 HCSB

Surely goodness and mercy shall follow me all the days of my life: and I will dwell in the house of the Lord for ever.

Psalm 23:6 KJV

I am not alone, because the Father is with Me.

John 16:32 HCSB

Putting God First

You shall have no other gods before Me.

Exodus 20:3 NKJV

Be careful not to forget the Lord.

Deuteronomy 6:12 HCSB

It is good to give thanks to the Lord, and to sing praises to Your name, O Most High; to declare Your lovingkindness in the morning, and Your faithfulness every night.

Psalm 92:1-2 NKJV

Love the Lord your God with all your heart, with all your soul, and with all your strength.

Deuteronomy 6:5 HCSB

The Devil said to Him, "I will give You their splendor and all this authority, because it has been given over to me, and I can give it to anyone I want. If You, then, will worship me, all will be Yours." And Jesus answered him, "It is written: You shall worship the Lord your God, and Him alone you shall serve."

Luke 4:6-8 HCSB

Happiness

How happy are those whose way is blameless, who live according to the law of the Lord! Happy are those who keep His decrees and seek Him with all their heart.

Psalm 119:1-2 HCSB

If they serve Him obediently, they will end their days in prosperity and their years in happiness.

Job 36:11 HCSB

The one who understands a matter finds success, and the one who trusts in the Lord will be happy.

Proverbs 16:20 HCSB

Happy are the people whose strength is in You, whose hearts are set on pilgrimage.

Psalm 84:5 HCSB

How happy is the man who does not follow the advice of the wicked, or take the path of sinners, or join a group of mockers!

Psalm 1:1 HCSB

A joyful heart is good medicine,
but a broken spirit
dries up the bones.

—

Proverbs 17:22 HCSB

Generosity

Based on the gift they have received, everyone should use it to serve others, as good managers of the varied grace of God.

1 Peter 4:10 HCSB

In every way I've shown you that by laboring like this, it is necessary to help the weak and to keep in mind the words of the Lord Jesus, for He said, "It is more blessed to give than to receive."

Acts 20:35 HCSB

Cast your bread upon the waters, for you will find it after many days.

Ecclesiastes 11:1 NKJV

Therefore, as we have opportunity, we must work for the good of all, especially for those who belong to the household of faith.

Galatians 6:10 HCSB

Each person should do as he has decided in his heart—not out of regret or out of necessity, for God loves a cheerful giver.

2 Corinthians 9:7 HCSB

All goes well for those who are generous, who lend freely and conduct their business fairly.

—

Psalm 112:5 NLT

Depend on the Lord and his strength;
always go to him for help.
Remember the miracles he has done;
remember his wonders and his decisions.

—

Psalm 105:4-5 NCV